The American Law School and the Rise of Administrative Government

The American Law School and the Rise of Administrative Government

WILLIAM C. CHASE

THE UNIVERSITY OF WISCONSIN PRESS

Published 1982

The University of Wisconsin Press
114 North Murray Street
Madison, Wisconsin 53715

The University of Wisconsin Press, Ltd.
1 Gower Street
London WC1E 6HA, England

First printing

Printed in the United States of America

For LC CIP information see the colophon

ISBN 0–299–09100–7

to the memory of
Louis Morton
from a student

Contents

Preface

This book had its genesis some fifteen years ago in my student experience at the Harvard Law School. There was little of the stuff of scholarship in my impressions and sensibilities of that period, but a skepticism about the ways and means of legal education took root in my first year of law school, endured over the years, and now informs—in some ancestral way—the arguments and suggestions of these pages. At the level of argument, this study will argue:

—that American legal scholarship has been heavily influenced by the configuration of its institutional home, the law school;
—that this configuration took shape under dubious circumstances at the beginning of this century and has never been adequate to the task of producing scholars for a modern society;
—that legal scholarship in turn has influenced American government, primarily by its insistence that a judicial model of decision-making has little applicability to the work of administration; and
—that this in turn has weakened the exercise of both administration and the judicial function in modern America.

And at the level of suggestion, it will attempt to suggest:

—that the law school has served us poorly in this century, and that it must be overhauled if it is to serve us better in the future; and
—that since the failures of American government in this century are attributable at least in some respects to the actions of this external agent, those failures have not taken the measure of government's possibilities.

More than skepticism supports these assertions, of course. But the reader probably has gathered from the size of this study that it stops short of being a comprehensive history of the American law school, of legal scholarship, or of administrative government. The reasons are, on the legal side, that it doesn't need to be comprehensive, and, on the administrative side, that it couldn't be. The principal contributions of legal scholarship to the growth of modern administration have come from the nation's leading law schools, especially the Harvard Law School. In terms of scholarly influence, this small community is American legal education. The study of administrative government, however, has no such unity about it. A single administrative agency or department produces enough materials to keep a researcher occupied most of his lifetime. And beyond that single administrative experience lie hundreds upon hundreds of others, each to some degree unique in its mandate, in its composition and structure, and in the economic, political, and social environments in which it operates.

I realize that when an author forsakes a comprehensive narrative of his subject he also forsakes the means to persuade his readers that his conclusions are ironclad. My hope, however, is that I can persuade readers of this work of the plausibility, if not the certainty, of its angle of vision, and stimulate further inquiry and argument about its concerns.

More people than I could have imagined several years ago have examined various versions of this study, and I have benefitted from their reactions, however communicated, whether they realize it or not. In particular, I wish to thank four persons for their criticism and encouragement along the way: Stephen Botein, Ernest May, Abigail Thernstrom, and Stephan Thernstrom.

Finally, to Frank Freidel there is owing more than just thanks, for his example and support have sustained a student's aspirations and hopes for the academic life in the face of it all.

The American Law School
and the Rise of
Administrative Government

Introduction

1

At present American legal thought is going through one of its periodic debates on the nature, purpose, and legitimacy of the judicial function. What seems to be emerging is a sense of a "modern" judicial function that is a dramatic departure from previous thinking. Whereas in the "traditional" view the judge's role was relatively passive, a mere adjunct to the efforts of private parties to order their affairs, in the modern view the judge has become an aggressive public "policy planner and manager."[1] The center of gravity of judicial business has shifted increasingly from retrospective questions of private law—whether, for instance, party *A* broke his contract with party *B* last year—to prospective questions of public law and policy—how a legislative purpose of the state may best be effected in the near future.[2]

That our sense of justiciable questions has grown so dramatically is due in part to the problems of late twentieth-century society that other branches of government seem reluctant to address, and in part to the discovery of certain institutional advantages of courts, in comparison with other agencies of government, for dealing with issues of public policy. Courts with their formal and adversary procedures are hardly ideal instruments *in the abstract* for effecting public policy, but they seem articulate, purposeful, and relatively immune to petty political influence in comparison with contemporary administrative agencies, executive departments, and legisla-

1. Abram Chayes, "The Role of the Judge in Public Law Litigation," *Harvard Law Review*, 89 (1976): 1302.

2. Ibid., 1284; for somewhat different statements of the transformation, see Donald L. Horowitz, *The Courts and Social Policy* (Washington: The Brookings Institution, 1977), 4–9; and Owen M. Fiss, "The Supreme Court, 1978 Term–Foreward: The Forms of Justice," *Harvard Law Review*, 93 (1979): 35–36.

tures. Even in terms of representativeness, an appointive, life judiciary fares well in practice, if not in democratic theory, against bureaucracies and legislatures. No one is particularly delighted with this result—our ingrained loyalty to the ideal of representative and responsive government tells us that there ought to be something better—but the result remains: in mundane, day-to-day, practical terms, courts hold up well. And while quite a few observers believe that this insight has been overextended, to the point of judicial usurpation, it seems unlikely that the judge's role in society will ever revert to what it was in an earlier day.[3]

This "modern" assessment of the possibilities of the judicial function did not come about overnight. Indeed, it has been a century in the making. But not until recently has even a rough synthesis been possible, so that only today can we visualize a "traditional" model and a "modern" model standing far apart on such questions as justiciability.[4] The reason, it is believed, that this synthesis could only begin to emerge after decades of piecemeal development is that the traditional model was firmly rooted in the realities of the world of seventy-five years ago. Legal thinking, political realities, and societal needs simply barred until recently the possibility that the judge would operate effectively as a policy planner and manager.[5]

But is this perception correct? One purpose of this study is to suggest that it is not. Rather, the suggestion here is that our "modern" sense of the judicial function was deliberately held up for more than half a century by the very persons who were entrusted by the legal profession and the American people with defining and publicizing new legal developments. These were legal scholars, located in the university law schools.

It is possible, of course, that even had the contribution of turn-of-the-century legal scholars been different, the behavior

3. Chayes, "The Role of the Judge," 1304–16; Fiss, "Forms of Justice," 28–44; Horowitz, *Courts and Social Policy*, 17–19, 255–98.

4. Chayes, "The Role of the Judge," 1285–1304.

5. Ibid., 1285–88.

and performance of judges would not have been. But I believe otherwise. For it should be realized that the full impact of our "modern" sense of the possibilities of the judicial function would not have been felt so much by the regular courts as by the then emerging "administrative process." This term describes the hundreds of agencies, commissions, boards, and bureaus that today oversee and police the details of our existence.

Today, the work of this process is regarded as pretty much separate and distinct from that of the courts. But if legal scholars at the turn of the century had popularized their sense of the judicial function—a sense that was very close in many respects to our "modern" one—it is credible, if not certain, that we would have seen a dramatically altered development of American administrative government in this century. Today, we would speak frequently, if not exclusively, of administrative courts and administrative jurisprudence, and our understanding of both the limits and the possibilities of the public policy function of the judge would be many decades old instead of only just emerging.

2

To clarify and elaborate upon these assertions, let us look first of all at the state of administrative government at the beginning of this century. American politics was groping for new methods of governing society, and in a general confusion of purposes at least one stood out clearly. This was to avoid the problems that were involved in the judicial enforcement of regulatory statutes.

In the nineteenth century, the usual method of dispensing the remedial power of government had been for the legislature to express its will in a statute and then trust private parties to enforce it by permitting them to sue for statutorily created rights in courts of law. For example, the legislative purpose that carriers should charge reasonable rates for their services would be effected by permitting shippers who had paid higher rates to sue for damages. But as one reformer noted, if "the vaunted common law was strong in name," it was "a shambling thing in action."[6] Exorbitant rate structures might continue unabated for months and years after the legislature had acted, while the courts sifted through the claims and counterclaims of witnesses and the motions and appeals of attorneys. Furthermore, a final court decree holding that a rate for a particular service was unlawful under the statute did not determine the legality or illegality of rates for related services. Each instance of alleged wrongdoing had to be litigated through a drawn-out process of trial and appeal.[7]

In a society that increasingly complained about the distresses of an industrial age, such slow and fractional enforcement seemed intolerable. The incapacity of the courts for effective regulation came to be perceived as inherent to some degree in any process that relied on private initiative and adversary procedures to achieve its results. At the same time, it was recognized that this problem was exacerbated by a generation of judges and practitioners who seemed too often learned only in archaic rules of procedure and a jurisprudence better suited to the conditions of a preindustrial society. Their torturous proceedings seemed to lead not infrequently to decisions that elevated an abstract individual liberty above the alleviation of palpable group distress. Society's problems appeared too pressing to wait for the time when the judicial process might be expected to reform itself. It seemed better to seek an alternative method of effecting the legislative will.[8]

The development of the administrative agency as this alternative was initially the result of political happenstance. The administrative process had begun to be perceived as a distinct part of government in the final three decades of the nineteenth century with the creation of state railway rate commis-

6. Charles McCarthy, *The Wisconsin Idea* (New York: Macmillan, 1912), 35. "Common law" here simply means the court system.

7. Ibid., 34–35; Bernard Schwartz, "The Administrative Agency in Historical Perspective," *Indiana Law Journal*, 36 (1961): 267–68.

8. McCarthy, *Wisconsin Idea*, 41, 238–42; Dwight Waldo, *The Administrative State* (New York: Ronald Press, 1948), 79.

sions and, more particularly, the Interstate Commerce Commission. But the debates on regulation in the legislatures of this period reveal an utter conceptual confusion about what was being created and a lack of appreciation for the possible consequences of this confusion. The dominant factors were the need from the politician's standpoint to take some sort of action against a railroad power which the citizenry had come to see as overbearing, and the ever-present necessity of compromising on a bill in order to gain its passage. In terms of how the proposed agencies were to conduct the business of regulating railroads, the debates suggested a variety of functions ranging from specialized transportation courts to purely executive action under the control of one of the established executive departments. Whatever the final form of the bills, it was not assumed in any case that a particularly large addition had been made to the workings of government.[9]

What had resulted for the most part was the creation of semiautonomous boards of officers with an ill-defined mixture of powers. These powers were not used to noticeable effect for the remainder of the century. The state railway commissions and the Interstate Commerce Commission soon were regarded as inconsequential. But in the first decade of the next century these institutions would be invested with an intellectual justification which would perpetuate and multiply their form, and thus turn an apparent nineteenth-century misadventure into one of the twentieth century's great hopes.

By 1910, the method of intervening more directly and quickly than courts against industrial disorder was thought to have been found. This was the utilization of administrative agencies that would act as the legislature's agents against unlawful practices in advance of or to the exclusion of a judicial trial. Reformers, scholars, journalists, and politicians all be-

9. Albro Martin, "The Troubled Subject of Railroad Regulation in the Guilded Age—A Reappraisal," *Journal of American History*, 61 (1974): 339–71; Bernard Schwartz, ed., *The Economic Regulation of Business and Industry: A Legislative History of U.S. Regulatory Agencies* (New York: Chelsea House, 1973), 1:17–584; Robert E. Cushman, *The Independent Regulatory Commissions* (New York: Oxford University Press, 1941), 19–34, 37–68;

came caught up in examining the governmental potential of these previously unremarkable bodies. In contrast to the courts, it was suggested that administrative agencies would be able to monitor continuously the circumstances of industrial life by means of corps of inspectors and periodic investigative hearings. In this way they would know immediately about violations of the legislative will, and they would be empowered to enter orders against them on the spot. This process was to be facilitated by speedy, informal proceedings and by decision-making that emphasized common sense and expert discretion rather than the abstract, precedent-bound logic of the courts. After a time, the agencies' knowledge of the problems under their supervision might become so detailed and comprehensive that they could issue orders prescribing good business practice and thus prevent future violations. The sporadic, contentious, and rule-clogged enforcement of the courts would give way to a continuous and frictionless expertise capable of responding to the new industrial world in its entirety and keeping pace with its ever-changing relationships.[10]

As an agent of the legislature, the administrative agency constitutionally would carry on this work independently of the judicial branch of government. The courts might step in to ensure that an agency was using fair procedures and no more power than the legislature specifically had given it, but, as in the case of the judicial review of legislative action, the substance of the agency's work was not to be inquired into. In conjunction with the legislature, the new industrial order was for the agency to effect.[11]

In actual practice, however, administrative agencies spent much of their time and resources imitating courts. Although

---

James E. Anderson, *The Emergence of the Modern Regulatory State* (Washington: Public Affairs Press, 1962), 79.

10. Robert H. Wiebe, *The Search for Order, 1877–1920* (New York: Hill and Wang, 1967), 133–63; Charles Evans Hughes, *Addresses and Papers, 1906–1908* (New York: Putnam, 1908), 93–94, 102–11, 141; McCarthy, *Wisconsin Idea*, 41, 46–47; A. A. Berle, "The Expansion of American Administrative Law," *Harvard Law Review*, 30 (1917): 430–48.

11. Bruce Wyman, *Principles of Administrative Law* (St. Paul: Keefe-Davidson, 1903), 13, 85, 154; Hughes, *Addresses and Papers*, 105–7.

the agencies had large staffs that the courts lacked, staff members seemed preoccupied with the ordinary routines and paperwork that accompany bureaucratization. Direct and immediate intervention against wrongdoing rarely occurred, orders prescribing future good practices rarely were issued, and the agencies usually waited for individuals to bring violations to light by means of complaints. Complaints initiated agency hearings and these were followed by orders granting or denying relief to the complainant. In terms of governmental function, what administrative agencies were doing was adjudicating controversies. In terms of the effective enforcement of regulatory statutes along these lines, the courts could have done no worse since they did the same thing.[12]

That is not to say, however, that there was no basis for a new and separate process of government in the early twentieth century. As we shall see, many administrative tasks were not justiciable. But to the extent that the administrative process merely withdrew issues from the jurisdiction of the courts—an early twentieth-century reaction against supposed judicial conservatism—and, more important, worked to divert justiciable controversies of twentieth-century origin away from the courts, the shift to administrative regulation entailed serious losses relative to judicial regulation. Because adjudication by administrative agencies was thought to be part of a new and different process of government, judicial standards of rational definition in issue-framing and decision-making did not pertain. This, as much as the relative novelty and complexity of the controversies that confronted administrators, accounted for what soon became characteristic of administrative adjudication: its rambling, lengthy hearings and its ambiguous and often irrelevant decision-making. The administrative function often was only the judicial function used unprofessionally.[13]

12. William E. Mosher and Finla G. Crawford, *Public Utility Regulation* (New York: Harper, 1933), 34–39; Schwartz, "Administrative Agency in Historical Perspective," 270–72; Martin Shapiro, *The Supreme Court and Administrative Agencies* (New York: Free Press, 1968), 91–93.

13. John Dickinson, *Administrative Justice and the Supremacy of Law in the United States* (Cambridge: Harvard University Press, 1927), 6–7, and

What had made administrative agencies appear to be wholly different from courts was their *potential* for continuous supervision and direct intervention. As a matter of professional tradition and for lack of resources, courts could not act without the existence of an actual controversy between parties litigant. Because it was assumed that agencies would be in constant touch with regulatory problems, it was also assumed that they soon would know more about these problems than not only a court but also the legislature itself. Therefore, it seemed futile for the legislature to prescribe a detailed plan of regulation for an agency to administer. It seemed better just to give the agency the power to act and let it work out the details on the job.[14]

Besides its apparent reasonableness, this approach was highly attractive to legislators who could now satisfy their constituents' demands for remedial legislation without voting for specific details that might offend some part of the constituency. The temptation to hand over some of the biggest problems before American politics to administrative agencies for both definition and resolution proved irresistible. But if these agencies indeed might have been able to enforce detailed statutory programs with greater directness and more continuity than the courts, they were almost helpless as *administrative* agencies to effect programs that did not exist. Their potential for speed and action compared to the courts was dependent on knowing in advance of a drawn-out trial what was wrong with society and what was to be done to correct it. Without this knowledge, the agencies' freedom from the supposed rigidities of the judicial process only fostered confusion. When the legislature told an agency simply to regulate business in behalf of an undefined "public interest," the agency was to issue immediately and in steady stream corrective orders against what practices?[15]

more generally, 8–31; Philippe Nonet, *Administrative Justice* (New York: Russell Sage Foundation, 1969), 235–37, 251–55.

14. Ernst Freund, *Administrative Powers over Persons and Property* (Chicago: University of Chicago Press, 1928), 28–30, 582–85.

15. Louis L. Jaffe, "The Illusion of the Ideal Administration," *Harvard Law Review*, 86 (1973): 1190; Grant McConnell, *Private Power and Ameri-*

The administrator of the early twentieth century had been thrust into a world of industrial disorder with power but not precept, and the function that his environment demanded was not unlike that, for example, of the itinerant justice who had been thrust into the feudal disorder of twelfth-century England. This was to arbitrate the most glaring disharmonies according to a rough sense of what behavior ought to merit the state's favor or disfavor. Lacking the ready-made definitions of good and bad that would have permitted an independent initiative against behavior perceived to be wrong, the power-bearer had to rely on the allegations of disputants to alert him to conditions that needed correction. In time, the English justices evolved beyond mere arbitration and sought to build from their resolution of disputes a comprehension of legal order. They sought a body of rules and principles that would have utility beyond the solution of one-time disputes. In this way also, they learned what kinds of controversies were unsuited to an adjudicatory process.[16]

In twentieth-century America, however, administrators consciously resisted building up a similar experience with the problems of regulation because they chose instead to chase the shadow of their expertise. Their rudimentary judicialism was a necessary retreat from administering a legislative program that did not exist, but further emulation of the courts was condemned in the name of all the hopeful theories that had accompanied the twentieth century's discovery of the administrative process. The predominance of adjudication in the work of administrative agencies was regarded as a temporary condition. After sitting through enough hearings, administrators would grasp the problems of regulation, and would begin to act in a truly administrative manner. Then would come the speed and the continuity of action and the prescription of social harmony. To be diverted from pursuing such a glorious

---

can Democracy (New York: Knopf, 1966), 38, 43; Glendon Schubert, *The Public Interest* (Glencoe, Ill.: Free Press, 1960), 198–224.

16. Sir Frederick Pollock and Frederic William Maitland, *The History of English Law*, 2nd ed. (1898; Cambridge: Cambridge University Press, 1968), 1:155–56, 2:670–72.

prospect for the sake of a glacier-like development of administrative precedents appeared only to invite the regulatory weaknesses of the nineteenth-century courts.[17]

A stage of true administrative "takeoff" was never attained, however. There resulted disappointingly little lasting experience, or broad comprehension, or even a sense of what kinds of disputes could or could not be adjudicated. The enforcement of regulatory statutes by the courts indeed had been unsatisfactory, but given the failure of the legislature to define in detail its regulatory purposes, administrative agencies could not hope to surpass the courts as regulators by practicing a primitive judicialism. The building up of experience through administrative precedents did not require the agencies to become courts in all things, but it did require them to take their decisions seriously and as useful guides in the justiciable portion of their work. Without this experience, the point of administration would not be reached, nor would there come from the administrative process any mature appreciation of the public policy functions of the judge.[18]

3

[T]here is building up a definite body of administrative law in this country, calling for systematic study and for conscious direction, so as to fit it into the general structure of Anglo-American law, and yet give it its appropriate scope, with the forms and procedure adapted to it. To do all this requires the sympathy and understanding of the Bar with the conditions and needs which have given rise to the development of administrative law with us, and the intellectual hospitality of the profession to the legitimate scope and aims of administrative law.[19]

When he wrote this passage in the early 1920s, Felix Frank-

17. Waldo, *Administrative State*, 79; Mosher and Crawford, *Public Utility Regulation*, 34–40; Nonet, *Administrative Justice*, 3–4.

18. Freund, *Administrative Powers*, 583; Louis J. Hector, "Government by Anonymity: Who Writes Our Regulatory Opinions?" *American Bar Association Journal*, 45 (1959): 1260, 1263.

19. Felix Frankfurter to William D. Guthrie, December 22, 1922, Frankfurter MSS, box 188, folder 3, Harvard Law School Library.

furter was a professor at the Harvard Law School and a leading authority on the administrative process. For the lay reader, his words seem to suggest that administrative decision-making is to some degree a judicial task, although not one for the regular courts, and that lawyers should take an interest in the decisions of administrative agencies in ways similar to their interest in court decisions. Indeed, as we shall see, this was a conclusion that legal scholars including Frankfurter had formed over the preceding two decades in the course of inquiries into the nature of law and the judicial function.[20]

Of course, given the regulatory shortcomings of the courts in the early twentieth century, this might seem to be a dangerous course. As Frankfurter's Harvard Law School colleague, Roscoe Pound, had observed in 1908, neither the judge nor the practitioner of this period seemed able to appreciate that the value of law lay in "the results it achieves, not . . . the niceties of its internal structure."[21] The quest for the appearance of logical certainty was plainly unsuited to solving novel regulatory problems, and it therefore seems possible that a substantive administrative law would simply have mired the administrative process in a mass of precedents.

However, an investigation of lawyers at work in the administrative process will suggest a potential in the profession even at this early date for developing an administrative jurisprudence suited to the needs and responsibilities of administrative government. And if this was so, then Frankfurter's call seems to augur much. For the lawyers of the early twentieth century dominated the administrative process. They held the majority ot upper-level agency posts, monopolized the role of advocate at hearings, and as judges of the reviewing courts had the power to make administrative practices conform to their liking. And in all this, they were willing to be guided by the scholarship of people like Frankfurter.

Whenever the legal profession—practitioners, judges, and

20. Full documentation for the assertions of sections 2 and 3 will accompany the text that enlarges upon them, i.e., chaps. 1–4, below.

21. Roscoe Pound, "Mechanical Jurisprudence," *Columbia Law Review*, 8 (1908): 605.

scholars—has been united behind a proposition that appears to turn upon legal understanding, the American people have invariably deferred, no matter how politically unpalatable the result. In other words, the relatively low regard for "courts" in the Progressive Era should not have prevented the rise of administrative courts if that had been the desire of a united legal profession, presenting the matter as one of legal necessity, correctly interpreted.

Why, then, did administrative courts and an administrative jurisprudence not arise? Because, as a lawyer would know, Frankfurter's meaning in this passage leads away from what, to the layman, is the apparent sense of his words. As Frankfurter would have the reader understand it, "administrative law" has nothing to do with the substance of administrative decisions. Rather, the term is meant to refer to what courts do in relation to administrative action, and as in the case of legislative or executive action, this is to review its basic legality but not its substantive content. "Administrative law" is confined to questions of fair agency procedures and the proper delegation of power from legislatures to agencies, and to rules of judicial housekeeping which determine under what circumstances the courts will review agency decisions on these questions.

Given this meaning for administrative law, the passage becomes what Frankfurter intended it to be, an appeal to lawyers not to hold administrative agencies to the standards of reasoned policy development that they expect of the courts. Lawyers should participate in the administrative process as agency members and as counsel at hearings, but always with an "intellectual hospitality" toward the tribulations of administrative expertise.[22]

Frankfurter's conception of an administrative law that ignored the substance of administrative decision-making was the accepted one in his time and it still is today. Like Frankfurter, most of the legal scholars who shared it might be regarded as caught up in the general expectation of the early

22. Frankfurter to Guthrie, December 22, 1922 (quotation).

decades of this century that administrative expertise was about to transform society. They did not wish to be narrow partisans of the values of their profession, and in their scholarship they chose instead to work around the edges of the administrative process at the points where a court might occasionally review an administrative decision. Indeed, they and the lawyers they influenced were among the most important expounders and developers of the idea of an administrative expertise. At the edges of the administrative process lawyers might engage in a strictly legal "systematic study and . . . conscious direction" of the court cases that dealt with the procedural context of administration. But all the rest called for only "sympathy and understanding."[23]

In a sense, then, legal scholars were simply beguiled by an exercise in overestimation that characterized the thought of their era generally. Moreover, it was apparent, then as now, that many administrative tasks could only be dealt with adequately through an executive, engineering, or technical approach, the more expert the better. But in another sense, in the sense that was closest to their professional consciousness, legal scholars were deliberately avoiding an area that they knew was ripe in many respects for higher judicial methods and the cultivation of their scholarship. For among the various expounders of the idea of a uniquely "administrative" expertise, they alone were in a position to know better. Since the late nineteenth century, they had been revising their ideas about judicial decision-making until they were at a point to see that judicial and administrative decision-making were often very similar functions.

Formerly, law had been thought of as a preexisting body of rules and principles from which a judge in his decisions merely selected the rule or principle that fitted the fact situation of the case at hand. Law existed ready-made and the judge was a searcher and finder of it in a rather mechanical fashion. A more creative conception of the judge's function, one of the judge as lawgiver, had never been entirely absent

23. Ibid. (quotations).

from legal thought, and in certain periods it had even been ascendant. But in the late nineteenth century the mechanistic view prevailed, and alongside it the crude arbitrations and makeshift accommodations of the administrative process seemed wholly alien.[24]

With no thought of drawing comparisons between the courts and administration, Oliver Wendell Holmes, Jr., in 1879 became the first of a growing number of legal scholars to react against the formalism of the mechanistic view. What he held to be a more realistic view of the judge's decision-making also described quite well the decision-making of the administrator:

> The official theory is that each new decision follows syllogistically from existing precedents. But as precedents survive like the clavicle in the cat, long after the use they once served is at an end, and the reason for them has been forgotten, the result of following them must often be failure and confusion from the merely logical point of view. . . .
>
> . . . The very considerations which the courts most rarely mention, and always with an apology, are the secret root from which the law draws all the juices of life. We mean, of course, considerations of what is expedient for the community concerned. Every important principle which is developed by litigation is in fact and at bottom the result of more or less definitely understood views of public policy.[25]

By the beginning of the twentieth century, Holmes' view of the judge as a policy-maker operating always with an eye to what is expedient was still too starkly stated for most lawyers. But the sense that he expressed of a judicial discretion to improvise in the face of changing conditions was gaining accept-

24. Fred V. Cahill, Jr., *Judicial Legislation* (New York: Ronald Press, 1952), 3–31; Calvin Woodward, "The Limits of Legal Realism: An Historical Perspective," *Virginia Law Review*, 54 (1968): 690–703; Lawrence M. Friedman, *A History of American Law* (New York: Simon and Schuster, 1973), 332–35, 591–92.

25. Oliver Wendell Holmes, Jr., "Common Carriers and the Common Law," *American Law Review*, 13 (1879): 630–31.

ance. This was so especially in the case of the scholarly lawyer who was a teacher in a law school.

As his conception of the judicial function came increasingly to resemble the expediential behavior of administrative agencies in deciding cases, and because those agencies spent much of their time deciding cases, the legal scholar could not escape the conclusion that the agencies possessed judicial power. It soon was accepted as irrefutable. But at the same time, the scholar denied that agency decisions should therefore constitute an "administrative law . . . calling for systematic study and for conscious direction" by the legal profession. Almost exclusively, court decisions continued to be the object of his study and his teaching. Because it had a wide currency in nonlegal thought, the idea of administrative expertise was a convenient device for justifying his court orientation. By blocking off the heart of the administrative process as something not strictly legal, expertise limited the extent to which the legal scholar had to incorporate administrative materials into the "general structure of Anglo-American law."[26]

4

To understand this curious compulsion, it is necessary to understand what was happening to the institutional context of American legal scholarship generally in the early years of the twentieth century. Formerly, judges had served as the shapers and systematizers of American law. But a modern society demanded ever more litigation, and increasingly the intellectual energy of its judges was being spent in deciding the narrow points of law presented by a growing caseload. Thus, to an observer such as Elihu Root it appeared that the newer and broader issues in the law were being given only "the impression of the moment."[27] There seemed to be missing any kind of "public opinion of the Bar" about "the broader consid-

26. Frankfurter to Guthrie, December 22, 1922 (quotations).

27. Elihu Root, quoted in "American Law Institute Is Organized," *American Bar Association Journal*, 9 (1923): 138.

erations of those relations which the profession of the law bears to the administration of justice as a whole."[28]

While Root along with many lawyers lamented this state of affairs, there were others who disagreed about the consequences of the judiciary's absorption in the narrow issues of the cases. It might be true, they said, that the newer fields of law would never again be developed adequately by those lawyers who were judges. But "the answer is that the new class of lawyers just emerging into group consciousness, the law teachers of the great universities, will ultimately rise to the accomplishment of this work of adaptation."[29]

Since the turn of the century, this assertion had been made with growing force and frequency, although the older leaders of the bar like Root had not heeded it. Only in the preceding decade had the law school begun to supplant law office apprenticeship as the accepted method of the lawyer's training, and the specialization of law teaching was a new and as yet a not entirely appreciated one within the profession. But having achieved "group consciousness" by 1900, law teachers entered a twenty-year period in which they claimed and won for themselves the role of the legal profession's opinion-makers on such questions as the nature of administrative decision-making.[30]

An address delivered in 1901 by the dean of the Harvard Law School, James Barr Ames, marked the opening of this period and set forth its arguments. Ames suggested that law teachers would not merely assume a function that judges no longer had the time for, but that they would discharge it with a thoroughness and competence which had not been seen before. The reason, Ames thought, was simple. As a scholar, the judge could never be more than a part-timer, whereas "the professor, on the other hand, while dealing with his subject in

28. Elihu Root, "The Layman's Criticism of the Lawyer," American Bar Association, *Reports*, 39 (1914): 391.

29. William R. Vance, "The Ultimate Function of the Teacher of Law," American Bar Association, *Reports*, 36 (1911): 763.

30. I derive the time frame for the professionalization of law teaching from Jerold S. Auerbach, "Enmity and Amity: Law Teachers and Practitioners, 1900–1922," *Perspectives in American History*, 5 (1971): 551–71.

the lecture room, is working in the direct line of his intended book."[31] In the period just ended, when law schools were few and law teaching was not yet a specialty, treatises had been written by judges, and while "some of our law-books would rank with the best in any country . . . as a class our treatises are distinctly poor. The explanation is to be found, I think, in the absence of a large professorial class. We now at last have such a class, and the opportunity for great achievements in legal authorship is most propitious."[32]

Of course, the decisions of the courts were still legally binding on any given point of law, but these could now be worked into comprehensive analytical systems by teacher-scholars. This process necessarily involved severe criticism of those decisions which did not fit neatly into a scholar's scheme of analysis. According to Samuel Williston, who had been one of Ames' students in the 1880s and was himself a great systematizer in the field of contracts, Ames "believed it to be the function of the lawyer, and especially of the teacher of law, to weld from the decisions a body of mutually consistent and coherent principles. To his mind there was but one right principle upon a given point, and if the decisions failed to recognize it, so much the worse for the decisions."[33] In this business of opinion-making, law teachers "proposed to lead rather than follow the judges."[34]

Law teachers were succeeding in their ambition to become the opinion-makers of the bar even at the time that Root was

31. James Barr Ames, "The Vocation of the Law Professor," *Lectures in Legal History* (Cambridge: Harvard University Press, 1913), 365.

32. Ibid.

33. Samuel Williston, "James Barr Ames—His Services to Legal Education," *Harvard Law Review*, 23 (1910): 332.

34. Alfred Z. Reed, *Training for the Public Profession of the Law* (New York: Carnegie Foundation for the Advancement of Teaching, 1921), 378 (quotation); for evidence of judicial assent, see Irving Lehman, "The Influence of the Universities on Judicial Decision," *Cornell Law Quarterly*, 10 (1924): 1–16; Benjamin N. Cardozo, *The Growth of the Law* (New Haven: Yale University Press, 1924), 14; and somewhat more generally, John W. Johnson, *American Legal Culture, 1908–1940* (Westport, Conn.: Greenwood Press, 1981), 52–68.

expressing his concerns on that matter. But to say that they supplied a "public opinion of the Bar" on issues that would otherwise have evolved more pragmatically and less analytically in the hands of busy practitioners and judges is not to say that this opinion always served to illuminate, in Root's words, "the broader considerations of those relations which the profession of the law bears to the administration of justice as a whole."[35]

In the field of administrative law, on the contrary, law teachers used their opinion-making power to obscure the implications of administrative decision-making for the legal order. The intellectual prestige that law teachers had acquired by forthrightly addressing some of the implications of the modern developments confronting the regular courts enabled them to persuade the legal profession to accept a view of administrative decision-making requiring only forebearance on the part of the courts, the law schools, and the bar.

The law teacher was committed to propagating this particular analysis as a public opinion of the bar. The cause of his commitment was the same as the source of his power to make opinion in the first place: the rise of the university law school. This event had called forth law teaching as a new legal specialty and had provided it with the resources and opportunity for scholarship which other legal specialties could not match. But the location of modern legal scholarship within the institutional context of the law school also set severe limitations on the nature of its inquiries.

By 1900, a narrowly conceived model of legal education associated with the curriculum and teaching methods of the Harvard Law School had come to characterize university legal education generally. This model was intensely committed to the study and teaching of the work product of the traditional courts, and it was just as intensely biased against the teaching of a topic like administrative law and against the study of the noncourt decisions which that topic's full scholarly development would require. This bias was always an unstated but

35. Root, "Layman's Criticism," 391 (quotations).

very real qualification to the sweeping assertions of the law teacher's scholarly and opinion-making roles put forward by teachers like Ames during the years between 1900 and 1920. The method of law study, teaching, and scholarship with which law teachers had succeeded first as law students and then as faculty members—in short, maintaining the status quo of their professional lives—was always more important than the pursuit of a true analytical scholarship. This would continue to be the essence of the matter after 1920, when the spell of Harvard appeared—superficially—to decline in the world of legal education.

What is being asserted here is not a conspiracy theory of legal scholarship. The scholars of the early twentieth century could not begin to imagine the importance that administrative government would assume in American life by the end of the century. The choices that they made for administrative government, in their writings, seemed to carry nothing like the consequences for later generations that have been suggested here. Thus, it is not necessarily a contradiction to find in Felix Frankfurter, for instance, both a passionate desire that the American experiment succeed and an inclination to obscure the judicial potential of the administrative process. In fact, as we shall see, the nature of the legal scholar's involvement with the set routines of his career was so strong that he could delude himself into believing that he was forthrightly seeking the truth in his scholarship, when in fact he was working diligently to obscure it.

Nevertheless, though legal scholars may have been nothing more than human in these efforts, the legal profession was not better off for having opinion-makers of this sort arise within it. Nor was American society. Legal scholars, of course, were but a small fraction of the total number of persons who put forward analyses of the administrative process at the beginning of this century. They were outnumbered by political scientists, journalists, and reformers of various persuasions. The initial formulation of the idea of an administrative expertise came from analysts of this sort and served, as we shall see, a variety of needs, real and imagined, in early twentieth-century society. But the writings of legal scholars were critical. They ensured that lawyers would not undertake to develop the primitive judicialism of the administrative process into anything more, and to say that lawyers would not do this is to say that it would not be done at all.

1

The University Prelude, 1870–1902

1

In 1870, a New York City lawyer named Christopher Columbus Langdell was appointed dean of the Harvard Law School. According to Ames, who was to be his pupil and his successor as dean, what Langdell found at Cambridge was "a school without examination for admission or for the degree, a faculty of three professors giving but ten lectures a week to one hundred and fifteen students of whom fifty-three percent had no college degree, a curriculum without any rational sequence of subjects, and an inadequate and decaying library."[1] Yet even this state of affairs was a considerable triumph for any law school in the period before 1870. The Harvard Law School was little more than a trade school, but one nevertheless that had been accounted better than its competitors by enough tuition-paying students to have assured its survival.

What Langdell inherited was a school that had originated a half-century earlier as merely an annual series of lectures given to the senior class of Harvard College and to members of the surrounding community. Its purpose was to inform them about the Constitution and law of the United States and to interest a few of them, perhaps, in a legal career. If such a career was eventually taken up, the instruction received at Harvard could be used to reduce the term of apprenticeship for becoming a lawyer. That a lawyer might acquire a part of his professional training at a college was pretty much an innovation, and one that would not succeed in ousting the pre-

1. James Barr Ames, "Christopher Columbus Langdell," *Lectures in Legal History* (Cambridge: Harvard University Press, 1913), 477.

dominant method of law office apprenticeship until well after 1870.[2]

If this early Harvard arrangement had suggested that legal education could be approached as an academic undertaking, it was soon terminated. In 1829, Joseph Story, associate justice of the United States Supreme Court, was engaged to give the instruction in law. He pushed legal education at Harvard in the opposite direction by breaking ties with the student body of the College and establishing an associated trade school without standards or examinations for admission or graduation. The aspirations of the curriculum were narrowed severely. It was Harvard that "lent the prestige of her name to the doctrine that calling a practitioner a university professor is equivalent to making his . . . law class a university school; and that an academic law degree may properly be conferred upon students entirely destitute of academic training."[3]

University legal education would never entirely shake loose from this approach, even after 1870. But in fairness to Story, it must be recognized that he taught in an era that was less hospitable to the idea of university-based legal training than that of the later nineteenth century. Story's school was supported solely by the tuition payments of its students, and it therefore had to be made as attractive as possible to students who had the option of entering the profession through doors other than the law school's. Whereas attractiveness might consist of a challenging academic regimen in an era when admission to the bar was difficult, Story's tenure coincided with a legislative trend in the Jacksonian era to weaken previously stringent bar admission requirements. In many states, periods of apprenticeship were shortened, and anyone, without any term of apprenticeship whatever, could be admitted to practice after passing an examination. Both the apprentice and the

2. Alfred Z. Reed, *Training for the Public Profession of the Law* (New York: Carnegie Foundation for the Advancement of Teaching, 1921), 112–41; Arthur E. Sutherland, *The Law at Harvard* (Cambridge: The Belknap Press of Harvard University Press, 1967), 37–91.

3. Reed, *Training for Law*, 140.

law student were now tempted to remain in their situations only long enough to acquire the practical skills needed to pass the examination, and the law school that desired to keep tuition-paying students in residence could not afford to enforce very demanding standards or offer more than a handicraft curriculum. At Harvard, eighteen months of study netted the degree, and only a year if the student had done work elsewhere. More stringent standards than these were thought to be "a little more than the traffic could bear."[4]

Joseph Story died in 1845, but the law school routine that he established was to persist for another twenty-five years. Students continued to enter and depart the Harvard Law School as they pleased, without the bother of formal evaluations. In the late 1860s, this state of affairs was being found wanting by an increasing number of observers. There was a growing feeling that the Civil War had ushered in a new and more demanding era in which lawyers would need better skills and higher standards of performance. It seemed evident that improving education at the Law School required the setting of standards for admission, student performance, and graduation, and that the best way to this was through competitive examinations. At the time of Langdell's arrival in Cambridge, the *American Law Review* presented a short, unsigned note composed by its co-editor, Oliver Wendell Holmes, Jr., which summed up this attitude:

> HARVARD UNIVERSITY. LAW SCHOOL.—For a long time the condition of the Harvard Law School has been almost a disgrace to the Commonwealth of Massachusetts. . . . [A] school which undertook to confer degrees without any preliminary examination whatever was doing something every year to injure the profession throughout the country and to discourage real students. So long as

4. Ibid., 179 (quotation), 167–68, 173–74; for more favorable views, see Gerard W. Gawalt, *The Promise of Power* (Westport, Conn.: Greenwood Press, 1979), 158; William R. Johnson, *Schooled Lawyers* (New York: New York University Press, 1978), 1, 20–23; Brainerd Currie, "The Materials of Law Study," *Journal of Legal Education*, 3 (1951): 362–67.

the possession of a degree signified nothing except a residence for a certain period in Cambridge or Boston, it was without value.[5]

Langdell proceeded to rectify the situation. In 1871, the residence requirement was raised from eighteen months to two years. In 1872, course examinations were instituted, with promotion to the second year and eventually graduation contingent upon passing them. In 1875, admission was limited to college graduates and to others who were able to pass an entrance examination. This examination presented difficult passages in French or Latin for translation and stiff doses of Blackstone's *Commentaries* for comment and analysis. The rigor of Harvard's requirements continued to increase until by the early twentieth century admission was limited exclusively to college graduates, three years of residence were required for graduation, and the course examinations had become occasions for intense competition and not infrequently the trauma of dismissal from the School.[6]

If for no other reason, the Harvard Law School graduate was good because he was select. Harvard's early leadership in educational requirements produced men who outshone both apprentices and the graduates of other law schools. By the 1890s, the performance of Harvard graduates had become widely recognized, and by the early twentieth century the Harvard Law School had achieved, according to Samuel Williston, "a clearer leadership in the field of legal education than any American institution of learning ever has had in its particular department."[7]

The institution of rigorous educational requirements by Langdell may properly be regarded as his fundamental reform

5. Quotation reprinted in Joel Parker, *The Law School of Harvard College* (New York: Hurd and Houghton, 1871), 3–4; for a defense of the status quo, see ibid., 16–21; also see Reed, *Training for Law*, 90–91, 141, 148.

6. Sutherland, *Law at Harvard*, 167–71.

7. Samuel Williston, *Life and Law* (Boston: Little, Brown, 1940), 206; Williston adds, ". . . with the possible exception for a brief period of the Johns Hopkins Medical School."

and the real foundation of Harvard's future success and influence.[8] According to Ames, the success of Harvard was Langdell's "chief ambition" when he came to Cambridge in 1870. "He wished to see it a great school in a great university."[9] But in Langdell's mind, such a development was not contingent simply upon the School maintaining scholastic standards superior to those of its competitors. He thought that higher standards would only make Harvard the best of the handful of law schools then existing, and these annually sought to stave off bankruptcy by attracting a few students away from apprenticeship and into their classrooms. What was needed in addition to higher standards was a compelling case for the importance of the university law school. At the time of his coming to Harvard, Langdell had been struck by "the anomalous condition of legal education in English-speaking countries . . . that in those countries a knowledge of law [has] been acquired in connection with its practice and administration, while in all the rest of Christendom law has always been taught and studied in universities."[10] What he wanted for the Harvard Law School was to give it the stature "occupied by the law faculties in the universities of continental Europe."[11]

For the eventual treatment of administrative decision-making by legal scholars, this could have been a very promising point of reference. In the course of the nineteenth century, the law schools of continental Europe had helped in the development of a system of administrative courts and a substantive administrative law.[12] But Langdell was inspired only by the prestige of the continental schools, and he borrowed noth-

8. Sutherland, *Law at Harvard*, 167–71.

9. Ames, "Langdell," 476.

10. Remarks of Professor Langdell, "Harvard Celebration Speeches," *Law Quarterly Review*, 9 (1887): 123; Langdell was talking about 1870.

11. Ibid., 124.

12. C. J. Friedrich, "The Continental Tradition of Training Administrators in Law and Jurisprudence," *Journal of Modern History*, 11 (1939): 129–48; Fritz Morstein Marx, "Administrative Regulation in Comparative Perspective," *Law and Contemporary Problems*, 26 (1961): 307–28.

ing from their methods or from the findings of their scholarship.

Instead, what Langdell did to try to make the Harvard Law School great was to make the study of actual court cases the basis of its instruction. Langdell's students were no longer assigned textbooks which summarized the law, but rather the actual cases in which its various rules and principles had been formulated. These were collected from the reports of decisions and reprinted for the student's use in "casebooks." This change had the effect of limiting the study of law to but one of its sources: the adjudication of the regular courts. In 1870, this "case method" was not the narrowing of the focus of legal education that it was to become after the rise of the administrative process. But Langdell did consciously exclude the study of legislation by means of this method, and it is clear from his later thought that he would not have considered administrative law a worthy subject for "law" study.[13]

Underlying this innovation was Langdell's expectation that the study of cases would benefit both the law student as a learner of the law and, more important, the law school as an institution "worthy of a university."[14] For the student, Langdell simply believed that the study of cases was more enlightening than memorizing rules divorced from the context of their evolution.[15] But the apprentice also read actual cases, and what, then, was the advantage for a law school in charging tuition for an experience which young men could encounter in a law office on salary? It was, according to Langdell, that what was learned by the study of cases in a law office could

13. Sutherland, *Law at Harvard*, 177–80; Robert B. Stevens, "Two Cheers for 1870: The American Law School," *Perspectives in American History* 5 (1971): 435–37; C. C. Langdell, "Dominant Opinions in England," *Harvard Law Review*, 19 (1906): 151–53.

14. Remarks of Langdell, "Harvard Celebration Speeches," 123.

15. See preface to C. C. Langdell, *A Selection of Cases on the Law of Contracts* (Boston: Little, Brown, 1871), reprinted in Josef Redlich, *The Common Law and the Case Method* (New York: Carnegie Foundation for the Advancement of Teaching, 1914), at pp. 10–11.

never be more than "a species of handicraft," whereas this same study carried on in a university could give rise to, and provide a mastery of, "one of the greatest and most difficult of sciences."[16] In a law office, the lawyer was motivated to take a report of decisions down from the shelf and hunt through it for a rule of law only when a client came in with some business. There was nothing more to it than that. But in a university, a law library containing all the reports of decisions of all the great jurisdictions of the Anglo-American world could be systematically explored by students and teachers alike for the sake of acquiring a scientific knowledge of the law. In a university, a law library is "the object of our greatest and most constant solicitude. . . . The library is the proper workshop of professors and students alike; . . . it is to us all that the laboratories of the university are to the chemists and physicists, the museum of natural history to the zoologists, the botanical garden to the botonists."[17]

It seemed to Langdell that "if law be not a science, a university will consult its own dignity in declining to teach it." But if it was a science, and if Langdell's experiment could demonstrate that "a university, and a university alone, can afford every possible facility for teaching and learning"[18] it, then the profession would have to consult its dignity in declining to recruit any longer its practitioners from among the ranks of apprentices; or from the graduates of law schools not following the case method.

Langdell proceeded with great confidence to the task of demonstrating the feasibility of his ideas. In 1871, he announced in the preface of his first casebook that it was "possible to take such a branch of the law as Contracts, for example, and, without exceeding comparatively moderate limits, to select, classify, and arrange all the cases which [have] contributed in any important degree to the growth, development,

16. Remarks of Langdell, "Harvard Celebration Speeches," 124.
17. Ibid.
18. Ibid.

or establishment of any of its essential doctrines." Given "the great and rapidly growing number of cases in every department of the law," Langdell realized that many lawyers would not regard this undertaking as possible, let alone capable of being confined to the "moderate limits" of a law school's academic year. But he believed that law regarded as a science yielded an insight into its nature that was missed by the practitioner who approached it as a business:

> Law, considered as a science, consists of certain principles or doctrines . . . [but] the number of fundamental legal doctrines is much less than is commonly supposed; the many different guises in which the same doctrine is constantly making its appearance, and the great extent to which legal treatises are a repetition of each other, being the cause of much misapprehension. If these doctrines could be so classified and arranged that each should be found in its proper place and nowhere else, they would cease to be formidable from their number.[19]

If the essential doctrines of any field of law were "much less than is commonly supposed," it followed that the cases illustrating them could be kept to a reasonable number for presentation to a law school class. The "cases which are useful and necessary for this purpose at the present day bear an exceedingly small proportion to all that have been reported. The vast majority are useless and worse then useless for any purpose of systematic study."[20] Thus, the law teacher would diligently sift the reports of decisions for the best cases, and the study of these by students would provide them with a scientific mastery of a field of law in a single academic year.[21]

But Langdell's "science" did not materialize from this process. The law's fundamental doctrines may have been few in

19. Langdell's *Contracts* preface, reprinted in Redlich, *Case Method*, at pp. 10–11.

20. Ibid.

21. For a catalogue of Langdell's pedagogic goals, see Preble Stolz, "Clinical Experience in Legal Education," *University of Chicago Conference Series*, no. 20 (1969): 58–72.

number as he believed, but their "different guises" were not easily penetrated. It became apparent that the kind of scientific mastery which Langdell believed "should be the business of every earnest student of law"[22] required the study of many more cases than a student could read in two or three years at law school. Harvard's casebooks were simply that: books of cases. The law student merely was exposed to some instances of adjudication, reprinted for his study. The older textbook system, while abstract, had at least attempted a comprehensive presentation. On the other hand, if one wished to study law by reading cases, at least in a law office one did so in a practical context, learning the rules of his particular jurisdiction as he went along. The cases for study at Harvard were not particularly useful once the student got into practice, for Langdell was inclined to choose outdated English cases that illustrated nicely a point he wished to make. According to Williston, he "derived the principles of his theology almost wholly from English cases, both because a thorough study of any fundamental legal principle in American law necessarily must go back to the English cases and because they were the one great common factor in the basic law of all the states."[23] These cases may have given some unity to Langdell's courses, but they were a very poor introduction to contemporary American law, and a far cry from the systematic mastery of it which had been Langdell's aim.[24]

This was not a system to impress the profession as making out a compelling case for university legal education. The reading of cases in a law school appeared to have little utility for practice, and it seemed to yield no more comprehensive or scientific knowledge of American law than that which the apprentice could pick up in a law office. Looking back on his student days at Harvard, one practitioner confessed that he had never been able to figure out "exactly what it was that the

22. Langdell's *Contracts* preface, reprinted in Redlich, *Case Method*, at pp. 10–11.

23. Williston, *Life and Law*, 200.

24. Stevens, "Two Cheers for 1870," 440; Redlich, *Case Method*, 41–47.

case method was supposed to teach."[25] It seemed to him that "in practicing law I very seldom get back to the point of view that the law school professors have."[26] Another critic was more blunt: "Those who go out and practice as client caretakers, as solicitors, play safe. They never for one moment think of resting the rights of their clients upon Harvard Law School law . . . they attempt to know what the Supreme Court of their state has declared. Are they in any position to impose Harvard Law School law on the courts . . . ? Not for one minute."[27]

Fifteen years after he had come to the Harvard Law School, Langdell's system of legal education had yet to make an impression on the larger world, except adversely. In 1870, Oliver Wendell Holmes, Jr., had applauded Langdell's introduction of scholastic standards and had predicted that his "labors will make the Harvard Law School what it ought to be."[28] But by the eighties, it seemed to Holmes that the additional innovations had been a "misspent piece of marvelous ingenuity."[29] In 1885, only 154 students were enrolled in the School, only slightly higher than the enrollment of 1870. And in 1886, Langdell's quest for a scientific mastery of law as the proper object of legal education was abandoned. This took the form of the abandonment of prescribed courses except in the first year. Since 1870, Langdell had been trying to build up a completely prescribed curriculum which would give the student a thorough knowledge of the law in all its important departments. Just as he expected to be able to select and arrange all

25. Remarks of Mr. [Herbert] Pope, "Papers and Discussion Concerning the Redlich Report," *American Law School Review*, 4 (1916): 108; Pope was Harvard Law School class of 1898.

26. Ibid., 109.

27. Remarks of Albert M. Kales, ibid., 111; also see Jabez Fox, "The Criticism of Cases," *Harvard Law Review*, 9 (1892): 200 ("what is this but a beating of the air?"), and Report of the Committee on Legal Education, American Bar Association, *Reports*, 15 (1892): 317–62.

28. *American Law Review* note, reprinted in Parker, *Law School*, at pp. 3–4.

29. Letter to Sir Frederick Pollock, April 10, 1881, *Holmes-Pollock Letters*, ed. Mark DeWolfe Howe (Cambridge: Harvard University Press, 1941), 1:17.

the important cases in the most profitable sequence for teaching particular subjects, so he thought that he could scientifically arrange all pertinent subjects within a curriculum. But the reading of cases yielded little mastery of particular subjects, and thus the subjects, however arranged, yielded no science. The whole scheme had shattered in the process of its implementation.[30]

In Langdell's mind, the study of cases had been the means for a law student to acquire a scientific mastery of law. But although such mastery faded as the goal of legal instruction at Harvard, the case method did not disappear. This resulted from the fact that law teaching had become a profession in the years since 1870. Claims in the status quo had been staked out by intense young careerists. Previously, lecturing to law school classes had been done by eminent judges and practitioners in their spare time or in their declining years of semiretirement. Story and his successors at Harvard to 1870 fitted this mold. But Langdell's dream of a science of law built upon the study of cases required a faculty that could devote itself full-time to mining the library for the cases that would best illustrate that science. It was a career in itself, and according to Langdell, "what qualifies a person . . . is not experience in the work of a lawyer's office, not experience in dealing with men, not experience, in short, in using law, but experience in learning law."[31]

Accordingly, in 1873 Langdell appointed one of his former students, James Barr Ames, to the faculty because Ames had been adept at the case method of learning law. Ames had never practiced law, had never been professionally outside the confines of the Harvard Law School, for, according to President Charles W. Eliot of Harvard, "Professor Langdell early

30. Stevens, "Two Cheers for 1870," 477; Reed, *Training for Law*, 308–9; Redlich, *Case Method*, 23.

31. Remarks of Langdell, "Harvard Celebration Speeches," 124; for a concise description of pre-Langdellian law teaching, see Lawrence M. Friedman, *A History of American Law* (New York: Simon and Schuster, 1973), 528–30.

advocated the appointment as teachers of law of young men who had no experience whatever in the active profession."[32] The foundation of Ames' career was what he had been able to do well as a student, that is, not master the law in its scientific entirety (for Langdell's curriculum failed to present this), or in its practical application, but master the skill of studying cases for classroom discussion. By the late 1880s, years of earnest labor had been devoted to researching and compiling casebooks for various courses, and an elaborate pedagogy had grown up around the study of cases. It was disappointing, perhaps, that a scientific mastery of law could not be imparted to students by this means, but too much was at stake now simply to shelve the whole apparatus.[33]

This retention of the case method was not necessarily cold-blooded. Indeed, there was an element of compulsive emotionalism in it. It has been said of the law teacher's student experience that "there is something self-confirming about [its] utility. . . . Professors tend to teach to and grade on the talents that made them successful law students."[34] Thus, Ames, who as a student had been able to analyze cases to Langdell's satisfaction better than other students, believed that the case method "was pre-eminently fitted for the cleverest men in the school."[35] Its value was further confirmed for him by his appointment to the faculty immediately upon graduation. So rewarded, Ames proceeded in his teaching to magnify the importance of his talent, and what he added to the art of the case method tended to make it even more self-confirming. Whereas Langdell assigned cases primarily for study, Ames initiated a classroom routine which, as described by an early twentieth-century practitioner of it, persists to the present day:

32. Quoted in Sutherland, *Law at Harvard*, 184.

33. Redlich, *Case Method*, 23; Sutherland, *Law at Harvard*, 183–91; Williston, *Life and Law*, 74, 76, 138–39.

34. Stolz, "Clinical Experience," p. 74, n. 67; the author is speaking about law review experience in particular, finding that "the academic kind of doctrinal analysis typical of student work in the reviews is nearly dysfunctional in law practice" (ibid., p. 74, text).

35. Ames, "Langdell," 480.

> This art or technique in general involves a discussion of the cases with different members of the class. It usually begins by one member of the class being asked to state the case. . . . The teacher . . . secures from the student a decided opinion upon the problem. Whatever it is, the instructor should be prepared to break him down. . . . If the instructor can break the student expert down and force a reversal of his opinion and then start in on him again and break him down a second time, so that he is forced to admit that his first opinion was right, the instructor will score a considerable success.

But this was not all:

> If the instructor can then go further and challenge any member of the class to produce a logical, workable hypothesis and if nobody can do so, and then if the instructor can himself produce a solution of the problem and in turn stand cross-examination, the session has been a decided success.

This case class was not something to be taken lightly. "The instructor must prepare definitely for this sort of cross-examining process. . . . he should put in a considerable amount of time and ingenuity in making that preparation."[36]

The emotional satisfaction to be had in teaching cases would have made it difficult to abandon the case method. From the 1870s to the present, for those few students whose mental processes meshed perfectly with the demands of the case class[37]—future law teachers, very often—the exhilaration experienced in being so clear-headed about what the teacher was driving at while all the rest of one's classmates foundered lasted for all their lives and confirmed their adherence to the Harvard Law School and its methods. One of Harvard's most

36. Albert M. Kales, "An Unsolicited Report on Legal Education," *Columbia Law Review*, 18 (1918): 22–23; for the importance of the case class for Ames in particular, see Thomas Reed Powell, "Law as a University Study," *Columbia University Quarterly*, 19 (1917): 117; remarks of Kales, "Papers Concerning the Redlich Report," 110. In some respects, Kales was quite critical of Ames.

37. It was said of James M. Landis, for instance, that "it seemed as if legal concepts came to him by instinct." Donald A. Ritchie, *James M. Landis* (Cambridge: Harvard University Press, 1980), 17.

legendary practitioners of the classroom ritual, Edward H. Warren, confessed at the end of his career: "What did the School do for me? I fell in love with the School at first sight, and that love still abideth with me."[38] In Felix Frankfurter, it evoked a "quasi-religious feeling."[39] In attempting to impose the case method on the Northwestern Law School in the 1890s, John H. Wigmore felt the emotions of "a legal missionary."[40] Besides the fact that careers had been built upon the study and teaching of cases, this emotionalism helped to save the case method.

How, then, was it saved? By repudiating that part of Langdell's educational objectives of 1870 directed to the attainment of legal knowledge. With those persons who still advocated it, Ames and his colleagues began "to differ radically as to the object of the three years at law school. . . . The objective arrived at by us in Cambridge is the power of legal reasoning."[41]

38. Edward H. Warren, *Spartan Education* (Boston: Houghton Mifflin, 1942), 6.

39. Harlan B. Phillips, ed., *Felix Frankfurter Reminisces* (New York: Reynal, 1960), 19. Although Frankfurter fell in love with the atmosphere of Harvard and Cambridge almost at first sight, academically he did poorly on his mid-year exams, and it was not until finals that he excelled. Thereafter he was, like Ames, confirmed in the belief that the methods of the Harvard Law School were calculated to uncover the cleverest men in the School. Ibid., 19, 26–27.

Readers who have difficulty believing that any pedagogy could produce such emotion, or that this emotion could be determinative of much of the structure of legal education, might wish to consult Scott Turow, *One L* (New York: Putnam, 1977). This is a vivid account of the student experience at the Harvard Law School in the mid-1970s, and it contains a number of shrewd guesses about what makes law professors operate as they do.

40. John H. Wigmore to James Bradley Thayer, May 6, 1894, J. B. Thayer MSS, box 18, folder 2, Harvard Law School Library. Wigmore provided Thayer with a running commentary on his early Northwestern adventures in several letters written during 1894 and 1895. Ibid.

41. Remarks of Ames, "Discussion of Paper by A. M. Kales," American Bar Association, *Reports*, 31 (1907): 1025. This conclusion began to be arrived at during the late 1880s; see Stevens, "Two Cheers for 1870," 440–41; and G. Edward White, *Tort Law in America* (New York: Oxford University Press, 1980), 28–29.

That Harvard did not impart a comprehensive view of the legal order should not be considered its failing. Rather, the law had grown too immense. It was, according to Ames' colleague, John Chipman Gray, "so enormously increased that its details cannot be known by any one man."[42] Therefore what was important, Ames suggested, was to provide students with an experience which would give them "the power of solving legal problems" once they got into practice, and "we think we can best get that by putting before the students the best models to be found in the history of English and American law . . . the opinions of the greatest judges that the English Common Law System has produced."[43]

The case method's critics should realize that this was the best result that university legal education could attain. Indeed, it should be recognized as vastly superior to the education of the apprentice whose reading of cases in a law office resulted in no more comprehensive knowledge (although he perhaps picked up a tradesman's grasp of the rules of his particular jurisdiction), and whose power to solve legal problems was not honed to a fine edge by the drills and competition of the Harvard Law School. If one overlooked the fact that Harvard's scholastic requirements guaranteed that its graduates would have innate ability, one could take satisfaction in the

42. J. C. Gray, "Cases and Treatises," *American Law Review*, 22 (1888): 759–60. Gray had not been one of Langdell's students, but he was very much one of the new breed of professional law teachers. Although he was slow to adopt the classroom dialectic, he was one of the earliest authors of casebooks. See Sutherland, *Law at Harvard*, 185; Williston, *Life and Law*, 74; remarks of James Bradley Thayer, "Section of Legal Education," American Bar Association, *Reports*, 18 (1895): 395, 402–3, 405–6.

43. Ames, "Discussion of Paper by Kales," 1025. This did not mean that Ames and his colleagues had arrived at a modern skepticism about the value or objective reality of formal legal rules. They simply had come to realize that the three years of law school were too short a time for the law student to comprehend more than a handful of formal legal rules by means of the case method. But for themselves, as legal scholars working over a professional lifetime, the quest for mastery of scientific legal principles would continue. See White, *Tort Law*, 31–37.

good showing that Harvard men increasingly were making in practice against lawyers trained by apprenticeship.[44]

The adherents of the case method, then, should not feel defensive about its utility for their students. But what about its utility for themselves as legal scholars? Langdell had sought to integrate scholarship and classroom instruction completely, with scientific casebooks as the intended result. If the casebooks now only presented examples of legal reasoning, law teachers on the basis of their classroom duties were nothing more than drill masters in the reasoning process. The conclusion was inescapable that scholarship, still questing after scientific mastery, had pretty much split off from teaching. But, Ames asserted, the classroom still might serve at least occasionally as a proving ground for an intended book, and in any case, law teachers were still better situated than other lawyers for devoting their spare time to scholarly endeavors. A profession of busy judges and practitioners ought to be grateful for any amount of light that law teachers might be able to shed on the ever-expanding mass of decisions. The more the profession supported the university law school as the proper mode of legal education, the more teacher-scholars there would be to carry on this useful work.[45]

In one sense, this transformation of argument on behalf of the case method was not particularly remarkable. In American higher education at the end of the nineteenth century there was a general shift away from the notion that mastery of a fixed body of knowledge was the goal of education in any discipline and a corresponding shift towards the notion that what was more important was to impart analytical skills and methodologies for confronting the almost indeterminate complexity of the "modern" world. Clearly, the Harvard Law School was

44. Redlich, *Case Method*, 23–28; Sutherland, *Law at Harvard*, 167.

45. Ames, "The Vocation of the Law Professor," *Lectures in Legal History*, 365; also see Thomas F. Bergin, "The Law Teacher: A Man Divided against Himself," *Virginia Law Review*, 54 (1968): 637–57.

part of this development.[46] But just as clearly, the fact remains that the ritual of case study was in place at Harvard, and generating career considerations, a decade and a half before its seeming rationale was discovered. Moreover, if the reasons for retaining the case method had not been convenient rationalizations in good measure, we should expect to have seen the study of administrative cases, as well as those of the regular courts, in the Harvard classroom after the turn of the century.[47] For a case is a case, regardless of where it originates—or at least it would have been treated as such if the case method had truly been only a classroom device for teaching problem-solving and analysis.

However, as much as the case method was a pedagogical device, it was a mechanism for the gratification of the professional law teacher. He wished to be true to the dimensions of the modern legal order, but not at the expense of destroying the institutional and emotional fabric of his professional life. The exhilaration of his student days—of being one of "the cleverest men in the school"[48]—had settled into a warm and lasting affection for the details of the law school experience, and particularly for the kinds of cases which had occasioned his early triumphs—that is, the cases of the regular courts, which were the only ones to be had in Langdell's day when the whole self-perpetuating mechanism began. The teacher-scholar's quick appointment to the faculty and successful career confirmed in his mind the utility of these things.[49] And the great danger of a true administrative law, of the study of administrators' decisions, was that ultimately it would push aside the study of the traditional subjects in the law school curriculum—because the decisional output of the administra-

46. Thomas L. Haskell, *The Emergence of Professional Social Science* (Urbana: University of Illinois Press, 1977), vi–vii, 20–21, 254–55; White, *Tort Law*, 23–31.

47. That is, assuming for the moment my assertion about the judicial potential of the administrative process is correct.

48. Ames, "Langdell," 480.

49. Stolz, "Clinical Experience," p. 74, n. 67.

tive process simply dwarfs that of the traditional judicial process. Whether consciously or perhaps subconsciously, the law teachers of the turn of the century could not bear the prospect that the traditional topics, the scenes of their early triumphs, ultimately would wither away—until in the entire three years of law school there might be only a handful of courses on traditional law, with the remainder devoted to the alien issues of the modern state.

In the coming century, law teachers would try their hands at scholarship and modify the offerings of the curriculum in order to acknowledge a variety of trends in legal education (optional fourth years, "law and the social sciences," realism, clinical education). But the core of the law school experience as Ames had encountered it as a student and then added to it as a teacher was to stay the same: the classroom cross-examination of students on *regular* court cases.[50] After all, the purpose of the case method, as John Chipman Gray liked to remark, was to teach "the student to consider law not merely as a series of propositions having, like a succession of problems in geometry, only a logical interdependence, but as a living thing."[51] It was a question of feeling and maintaining the sources of that feeling. "The acquisition of this attitude towards the law is likely to be deemed of fundamental importance according as a professor is a believer in the common law [i.e., judge-made law]. We are all here firm believers in it. We desire that the students may be filled with its spirit."[52]

In a sense, the ritual of the university case method was a mechanism of modern invention that assured that the traditional insularity of the common-law lawyer would survive into the twentieth century with none of its parochialism diminished. The study of administration might be a worthy scholarly endeavor in the law schools of continental Europe, but in America, except as it could be studied in the opinions of the

50. Joel Seligman, *The High Citadel* (Boston: Houghton Mifflin, 1978), 149–59.

51. J. C. Gray, "Methods of Legal Education—IV," *Yale Law Journal*, 1 (1892): 159.

52. Ibid., 156.

reviewing courts, it was to lie irretrievably outside the affections of the teacher-scholar.[53]

Thus, the men of the Harvard Law School were going to retain the case method, even though it did not impart a comprehension of the modern legal order, and they were going to confine the method to the study of the traditional courts. That resolve, of course, would not have counted for much if the Harvard Law School had remained the insignificant operation that it was in the 1870s and early 1880s. But by the end of the century, Harvard's enrollment had quadrupled and its model of legal education was becoming dominant.

It has been generally assumed that Harvard's sudden prosperity resulted from the merits of its instruction. But if Harvard's rise is placed in the context of the general rise of American higher education after the Civil War, its prosperity and influence will be seen to result from other forces almost entirely. The story of Harvard's institutional success does not support the conclusion that its educational and scholarly values fitted the needs of the legal order.

In the four decades following the Civil War, not just legal education at the Harvard Law School but American higher education in general was transformed. Before the war, insti-

53. In contrast to the foregoing interpretation, which locates legal scholarship's response to administration in narrow and compulsive institutional self-interest, one could try to take a view of the matter kinder to the Harvard men: that the late nineteenth century was an age of severe legal formalism, something that was hardly an invention of the Harvard Law School for its institutional convenience, and that made inevitable a detached and disinterested response by legal scholarship to administration. The problem with this view, however, is that legal formalism was in decline by the time that the issues of the rising administrative process presented themselves to legal scholars. See Introduction, sec. 3, above, and chap. 3, sec. 3, and chap. 4, secs. 1–2, below.

For a discussion of how an era of legal formalism almost inevitably sows the seeds of its own destruction, see Philippe Nonet and Philip Selznick, *Law and Society in Transition* (New York: Octagon Books, 1978), 53–72. The problem for the early twentieth century, I would argue, was that the institutional drag of the law school prevented the extension to administration of the new insights into the nature of law and the legal order.

tutions such as Harvard College had existed on very modest scales, with perhaps a struggling professional school or two associated with them. By the beginning of the twentieth century, they had become booming, multifarious universities. The first half of this forty-year period of transformation witnessed little material growth, but it was alive with experimentation and diverse proposals for change. Langdell was but one of many educators who captured a college president's fancy with a visionary scheme in this period. "Within the academic world, everything seemed uncertain. A number of alternative possibilities for growth and development had appeared,"[54] and men such as Harvard's President Eliot were not disposed to press for quick results from innovators like Langdell. It was enough that they spoke of such things as "science," the future greatness of the university, making teaching a true profession, and making their students into trained experts in a particular line of endeavor.[55]

Outside of the university, the larger world also was not disposed to inquire closely into these experiments, being then engrossed in a Gilded Age. "From the point of view of those who sought a distinctive role for the university, it was the best possible circumstance that higher education remained relatively unpopular for more than two decades after 1865. In this period the young university enjoyed a temporary (if partial) liberty of action."[56] The Harvard Law School in particular had time enough to discover the impracticalities of its methods, and if not eliminate them, at least discover reasons sufficient for retaining them. By 1890, those educational experiments which, like Harvard's case method, were still intact were to reap the benefits of a sudden boom in the fortunes of American higher education.

In the nineties, the university degree was becoming both a symbol and a means of advancement for members of a "new

54. Laurence R. Veysey, *The Emergence of the American University* (Chicago: University of Chicago Press, 1965), 56.

55. Ibid., 17; White, *Tort Law*, 6–26.

56. Veysey, *American University*, 17.

middle class" who "found their rewards more and more in the uniqueness of an occupation and in its importance to a rising scientific-industrial society."[57] Higher education had become a growth industry. In legal education, the rush to build or refurbish physical plants, curricula, and faculty was carried on with a boom psychology, and "once any one respectable institution moved in a new direction, others found themselves under a powerful compulsion to follow suit."[58] Furthermore, the profession at large, while it continued to be suspicious of the pedagogical value of the case method, was now anxious to acquire the prestige of being a university-educated profession. In particular, the spur of a great and somewhat earlier expansion in medical education and the medical profession's resulting prestige caused many lawyers to accept, for its symbolic value, a university legal education based on the case method.[59]

The boom of the 1890s was made to order for the Harvard Law School. For over a decade, Ames, who became dean in 1895, had been building up a corps of professional law teachers grounded in the case method. These men were now in demand by other law schools that wanted to replace the part-timers (practitioners and judges) on their faculties with professional teachers. Many universities also were opening or expanding law schools. "During my five years as an assistant professor," Williston later recalled, "I was offered the deanship of three law schools."[60] Like Wigmore at Northwestern, the other Harvard men who left Cambridge saw themselves as legal missionaries for the case method in their new surroundings. At Northwestern, for instance, Wigmore reported that

57. Robert H. Wiebe, *The Search for Order, 1877–1920* (New York: Hill and Wang, 1967), 129; also see Veysey, *American University*, 264–65; and Burton J. Bledstein, *The Culture of Professionalism* (New York: Norton, 1976), 38–39, 296–97.

58. Veysey, *American University*, 11.

59. Wiebe, *Search for Order*, 116, 121; Friedman, *History of American Law*, 526; an example is a letter from William Howard Taft to James Bradley Thayer, May 4, 1896, J. B. Thayer MSS, box 18, folder 7, Harvard Law School Library.

60. Williston, *Life and Law*, 140.

"there was a threatening of a storm. . . . But there was a general assault on the part of us all with the case method."[61]

The spread of the case method also could be effected in more subtle ways. Eugene Wambaugh, who was to have a long career at Harvard, wrote a little book, *The Study of Cases*, with the object that "wherever it is used it will be the thin edge of the wedge" for the introduction of the case method.[62] In addition, according to Samuel Williston, "the casebooks prepared by the Harvard professors contributed to this result."[63] Law schools wishing to sample the case method found that they had to swallow Harvard whole, because "there were hardly any [other casebooks] obtainable at first, and, until professors of other schools had had sufficient time to produce books of their own, the Harvard books were almost the exclusive basis for study and instruction."[64]

Just as important as these advantages to the case method's success was the selling campaign that Harvard men undertook in the nineties. Next to Ames, the most imaginative spokesman for the study of cases was William A. Keener, a young Harvard professor who went to Columbia in 1890. Keener suggested that it was "a curious contradiction that, at a time when it is universally recognized that the teaching of law is one of the functions to be discharged by a university, opposition should be raised to the adoption of a method of teaching law that is applied in nearly all departments of university work."[65] For any who might not have supposed that the case method was so widely regarded, Keener cited Herbert Baxter Adams' description of the graduate history seminar at Johns Hopkins, with its avoidance of textbooks and lectures and its

61. John H. Wigmore to James Bradley Thayer, May 6, 1894, J. B. Thayer MSS, box 19, folder 6; also see letters from Wigmore to Thayer of December 30, 1894, March 4, 1895, and June 1, 1895, ibid.

62. Letter to J. B. Thayer, February 17, 1892, J. B. Thayer MSS, box 20, folder 2.

63. Williston, *Life and Law*, 206.

64. Ibid.

65. William A. Keener, "The Inductive Method in Legal Education," American Bar Association, *Reports*, 17 (1894): 473.

emphasis on independent research and classroom discussions. "A higher authority than Professor Adams cannot be quoted, and a nearer approach to the case method of instruction cannot be found than the method described by him."[66]

In the boom times of the nineties, Keener's favorable comparison of the drills of the Harvard Law School classroom with graduate study in history at Johns Hopkins attracted the interest of the university president and his trustees who wished to vest their own institution with some of the stature then enjoyed by Johns Hopkins. They could not know the significance of Keener's immediate qualification to his comparison, that the law student's "investigations are made under the direction and with the assistance of his instructor."[67]

Not the relative merits of the case method but salesmanship was carrying the day. In the same article in which Keener compared the case method to instruction in the arts and sciences in the nation's best graduate schools, he assured practitioners that the case method simply dealt with "the practical side of the law."[68] But truth in advertising really did not matter. The surge in law school enrollments in the nineties combined with Harvard's exceptionally high scholastic standards to produce graduates with innate ability, and the dysfunctions of the case method were never so great as to break down the advantage of talent. The success of Harvard graduates in practice seemed to confirm the claims that were being made for the case method and, indeed, if the profession of law were to be regarded as only a nomadic journey from one legal problem-solving task to another, the case method as amplified by Ames' classroom drills probably was functional. All that was missing was a concern for a larger frame of reference. For the student who viewed his future as nothing more than, in Elihu Root's words, "the fee and the triumph in the particular case,"[69] this was not a problem. For the scholarship of his

66. Ibid., 474.

67. Ibid., 481.

68. Ibid., 483.

69. Elihu Root, "The Layman's Criticism of the Lawyer," American Bar Association, *Reports*, 39 (1914): 391.

teachers, however, it would prove to be a very serious problem indeed.

2

Harvard's sudden prosperity in the 1890s was all the more remarkable in light of the fact that the School, for all its seeming connection with the educational ferment of the time, was cut off from one vital source of inspiration for American higher education in this era. This was the model of the European, especially the German, university. Until the end of the century, its purposes and methods were powerfully in vogue among the personnel of the emerging American university. Langdell, of course, had been inspired by the prestige of the continental law schools, but beyond that he rejected them as models, and Ames was to follow him in this rejection. Harvard men were, as John Chipman Gray pointed out, believers in the common law and only the common law.[70]

Fundamentally, Harvard was having success exploiting the boom psychology of the nineties only because it did not have to compete with the example of another law school that more closely approximated the educational methods and purposes of the general university community. There were, however, American teachers of law in the 1890s who wished to borrow heavily from European legal education—"as nearly as the situation and public opinion in America would allow," according to the constitutional theorist Christopher G. Tiedeman. "This is the system which I learned to admire while sitting under the skillful instruction of the celebrated von Jhering of the University of Goettingen."[71] Law teachers such as Tiedeman shared an inspirational bond with other members of the university, and to this bond Ames and the Harvard Law School men were outsiders. In contrast to the case method teachers, the Europeanists were inspired by their foreign

70. Veysey, *American University*, 55; Gray, "Methods of Legal Education," 156–59.

71. C. G. Tiedeman, "Methods of Legal Education—III," *Yale Law Journal*, 1 (1892): 150, 151.

study to emulate the continental law school's comprehensive survey of the legal order, to the ends of both practical and theoretical understanding. That administration had a place in this survey was taken for granted.[72]

Interestingly, the Europeanists' goals elicited a favorable response from practitioners, who tended to identify university education in any discipline with the pursuit of understanding. In 1892, the Committee on Legal Education of the American Bar Association recommended "the abandonment of the present method of teaching the law mainly by distinct topics, at least during the first year . . . and the substitution for it of a careful and systematic study of the [legal] system as a whole after the European model."[73]

While this support was significant, what was essential for the triumph of this perspective was that it be institutionalized somewhere as had happened with the study of cases at Harvard. In order to exploit the boom of the 1890s, the example of a functioning law school and the missionary zeal of young teachers trained in its methods were required. And in 1894, such a law school began to evolve.

In that year, a young professor named Ernst Freund left Columbia to join the political science department at the new University of Chicago. At the time of his arrival in Chicago, the University was considering establishing some kind of program in legal studies, and Freund was determined to work for the creation of a law school emphasizing, among other things, the study of administrative government. With the rise of the administrative process in America, it seemed to Freund that such a school would not appear to be straying from the "strictly legal," but indeed would compare favorably with schools such as Harvard. The latter would increasingly be perceived as confining "its legal education to a professional training of a highly specialized type, overstressing the forensic at

72. Ibid., 150–58; Louis Wirth, "The Social Sciences," in Merle Curti, ed., *American Scholarship in the Twentieth Century* (Cambridge: Harvard University Press, 1953), 43; Redlich, *Case Method*, 40–47, 65.

73. Committee on Legal Education, 1892 Report, 360 (quotation); also see pp. 319–20, 340, 344, 348–50.

the expense of the administrative side of the law,"[74] and thus the theoretical foundation of Harvard's approach—that "our law is nearly altogether produced by our courts in deciding cases"—must inevitably collapse.[75] Freund believed that he could give to the law school envisioned for Chicago the leadership in legal education currently enjoyed by Harvard, and events over the next eight years were to prove him nearly correct.[76]

In his ambition, Freund was influenced by his experiences at Columbia, as well as his early upbringing. Intellectually, he looked toward both Europe and America. He had been raised in Germany and received his undergraduate and legal education there, earning the J.U.D. degree from Heidelberg in 1884. But he had been born in the United States during a visit by his parents in 1864, and in 1886 he moved to New York City and opened a law practice. After six years in practice, Freund joined the faculty of Columbia's School of Political Science as an instructor in jurisprudence and Roman law, and at the same time began work for a Ph.D. in political science. And it was at Columbia that Freund first realized the importance of an educational setting for the development of fields of law.[77]

The status of administrative law at Columbia was clearly unfortunate. The professor who taught it held a joint appointment in both the Law School and the School of Political Science, with the result that the subject seemed to belong properly to neither school. This was Frank J. Goodnow, who in 1893 had produced a landmark piece of scholarship, his

74. Ernst Freund, "Law School and University," *University* [of Chicago] *Record*, 18 (1932): 148; Freund was looking back to the turn of the century here.

75. Ernst Freund, "Political Science in Law" (undated manuscript, c. 1895), Freund MSS, box 2 addenda, University of Chicago Library.

76. For the discussions about legal education at the University of Chicago during the 1890s, see Frank L. Ellsworth, *Law on the Midway* (Chicago: The Law School of the University of Chicago, 1977), 30–47.

77. Frederic Woodward, "Ernst Freund," *University* [of Chicago] *Record*, 19 (1933): 39; comment, "Ernst Freund—Pioneer of Administrative Law," *University of Chicago Law Review*, 29 (1962): 755.

two-volume *Comparative Administrative Law*— the first attempt to state the relevance of continental administrative law to the rising administrative process in America. But due primarily to the orphan status of administrative law in Columbia's institutional scheme, Goodnow's effort was not noticed. To political scientists, it seemed "legalistic"—which it was—and was largely ignored by them, while lawyers could dismiss it as something not "strictly legal" because of its author's association with a school of political science. Although Goodnow gave instruction to law students that would have been regarded as strictly professional in the law schools of continental Europe, his political science connection made his interests appear to be peripheral to a lawyer's education. A Columbia law student of the early twentieth century later recalled that "long before I arrived in his class Goodnow had learned that he must concentrate on American administrative law, and his epoch-making volumes on comparative administrative law were never referred to except as an item in the bibliography announced at the first lecture."[78]

Goodnow was put off by this lack of response to his potentially ground-breaking work and by the procedural, appellate court focus that had to pass as administrative law in his teaching in order to get law students to enroll in his courses. After the mid-nineties, his scholarship edged away from a legalistic approach and toward political science and public administration. He despaired of lawyers ever realizing the substantive importance of administrative decisions unless one were allowed to "beat it into the heads of the legal profession."[79] But seeing the peripheral status of administrative law in the na-

78. Arthur T. Vanderbilt, "Introduction," in Bernard Schwartz, *French Administrative Law and the Common-Law World* (New York: New York University Press, 1954), xiii (quotation); for the Columbia situation, see R. Gordon Hoxie et al., *A History of the Faculty of Political Science, Columbia University* (New York: Columbia University Press, 1955), 5–19, 262; and Glendon Schubert, "The Future of Public Law," *George Washington Law Review*, 34 (1966): 593–614.

79. F. J. Goodnow, "Discussion," following Edmund M. Parker, "Administrative Courts for the United States," American Political Science Association, *Proceedings*, 6 (1909): 64.

tion's law schools, Goodnow felt that the opportunity was not likely to occur and that the best hope was "that somewhere . . . there should be established a school or department not for the education of lawyers for the practice of law, but for the study of jurisprudence." Then "greater attention might be given than is now possible to the solution of the many legal and political problems which the great changes in our economic and social life are with increasing emphasis bringing to our attention."[80]

When Freund had the opportunity to go to the University of Chicago in 1894, he took with him the lesson of the importance of institutional context for developing a field of learning. But he differed with his former colleague Goodnow on an essential point: the feasibility of teaching something like Goodnow's version of administrative law in a law school environment. Freund felt that from the standpoint of furthering the study of administrative law it would be a mistake to establish a school of jurisprudence rather than a true law school. For Freund, the future of administrative law depended on making lawyers realize that it truly was "law." He felt that this could be done by making administrative study an integral part of the instruction in an institution which was clearly a law school. Freund realized that in a law school, "law is not studied for its intrinsic interest," but primarily "as a means of earning a livelihood,"[81] and he was confident that administrative law could qualify as law on this count. His confidence stemmed from his first-hand knowledge of the law schools of continental Europe, which were "frankly professional schools" and yet studied administration in great detail.[82]

Within a year of his arrival at Chicago, Freund submitted a curriculum for a proposed law school to the University's presi-

80. Frank J. Goodnow, "Private Rights and Administrative Discretion," American Bar Association, *Reports*, 41 (1916): 423.

81. Freund, "Political Science in Law."

82. Freund, "Law School and University," 149 (quotation); also see ibid., 143–52; and Richard J. Storr, *Harper's University: The Beginnings* (Chicago: University of Chicago Press, 1966), 291–92.

dent, William Rainey Harper.[83] But the lack of an endowment and disagreement among the trustees as to whether they wanted a true law school or a school of jurisprudence delayed implementation of Freund's ideas for seven years. During this period, however, he began to develop his courses in the department of political science with an eye to their eventual incorporation into a law school curriculum,[84] and when in 1901 the University's trustees finally decided to establish a law school, he was ready. For some time, Freund had had President Harper's ear on this question, and in January 1902 he was authorized by Harper to draw up the curriculum for the new school. Written in consultation with Harper and political scientist Henry Pratt Judson, this was submitted in early March.[85]

83. Ernst Freund to William Rainey Harper, January 31, 1895, Presidents' Papers 1889–1925, box 19, folder 5, University of Chicago Library.

84. Freund's instruction in administration was markedly more legal in its emphasis than that of the other members of the department. He not only covered the organization of the administration, which was the seminal concern of public administration, but also such law-oriented issues as "control over the administration, its powers over the citizen, its forms of action, its liabilities, and the remedies against it." See course description in the University of Chicago's *Annual Register* for 1894–95; compare the nature of the instruction given in the following year by another member of the department, *Register*, 1895–96, at p. 65. The clearest example in this period of how Freund differentiated public administration from administrative law is found on p. 66 of the *Register* for 1895–96 in the descriptions of courses 35 and 36. Other Freund offerings of the period were on the nature of the judicial power in government and a course on comparative administrative law; see *Register* 1894–95, at p. 61 (course 27), and *Register* 1897–98, at p. 192 (course 28). By the end of the 1890s, in fact, the outline of Freund's later scholarship, particularly with regard to analyzing the relationship between administration and legislation and the ways and means of both, had begun to appear in these courses for the political science department; see *Register* 1897–98, at p. 192 (course 25), and *Register* 1900–1901, at p. 190 (course 26). For the event that precipitated all this development within the confines of the political science department, the failure to implement Freund's 1895 law curriculum proposal, see Ellsworth, *Law on the Midway*, 39–40.

85. Freund's curriculum is found with a cover letter to Harper of March 9, 1902, Presidents' Papers 1889–1925, box 34, folder 17; background is

Freund's plan placed the study of administration on an equal footing with the more traditional legal topics. Administrative law at Chicago was to be taken in the second or third year under an elective system that required a student to take at least four courses in public law and jurisprudence. By contrast, administrative law at Harvard was not an offering for the LL.B. until the 1940s, and jurisprudence was barely tolerated as something not really pertinent to training for a practical profession. Freund intended personally to teach a substantial number of first-year courses in traditional subjects, which suggests that he meant to ensure that the students would not acquire biased attitudes toward administrative law from their traditional classes, as he had seen happen at Columbia. As for the case method, it was to be used only to the extent that it did not impede a student's ability to comprehend systematically the subject being studied.[86]

Thus, in early March 1902 it appeared that the University of Chicago was moving toward presenting a striking alternative to the Harvard Law School's approach to legal education. Freund's plan represented an important challenge, for according to Harlan F. Stone, the case method could not have been triumphant until Chicago fell into line.[87] But Freund himself

found in Storr, *Harper's University*, 292–93; and in Ellsworth, *Law on the Midway*, 48–63; also see Freund to Harper, April 24, 1901, Presidents' Papers 1889–1925, box 19, folder 5; Harper to Freund, January 9, 1902, ibid.

86. For Freund's use of cases, see Paul L. Sayre, "A Common Law of Administrative Powers," *Iowa Law Review*, 18 (1933): 242–44; Harvard's approach to public law is discussed in S. P. Simpson, "The New Curriculum of the Harvard Law School," *Harvard Law Review*, 51 (1938): 980; if a student wished to take a public law course before the third year, he had to secure administrative permission; on jurisprudence, see remarks of James Barr Ames, "Discussion of President's Address," American Bar Association, *Reports*, 26 (1903): 663–64.

87. Harlan F. Stone, "Dr. Redlich on the Case Method in American University Law Schools," *Columbia University Quarterly*, 17 (1915): 262; by this time, Stone was dean of the Columbia Law School.

was the cause of Chicago's fall into Harvard's orbit. For some time, Freund had been advising President Harper to consult Ames for suggestions "about young men of promise who are qualified to teach law, and his general ideas on a law school."[88] Freund appears to have been motivated by his overriding concern that the new Chicago Law School be perceived as "frankly professional"[89] even though it emphasized the study of administrative law and jurisprudence. "It was not chiefly or primarily the method of instruction which had become identified with the name of Harvard that challenged admiration," he would later recall, "but the spirit of earnestness and devotion to their chosen work on the part of the students." Freund deemed it "essential to transplant and reproduce" this spirit in students who would be engaged in the study of both traditional and modern legal topics.[90]

Negotiations between Harper and the Harvard administration quickly resulted in an agreement to bring to Chicago a Harvard Law School professor, Joseph H. Beale, to serve on a temporary basis as the dean of the new law school. Since Freund had control of the curriculum and was President Harper's closest advisor on issues concerning the law school, he may initially have had no reservations about Beale's suggestion to Harper "to induce a dozen men, perhaps, graduates of your university, to leave our school for a couple of terms and go to the new school, hoping thereby to start with the right spirit and get tradition established there."[91] At the end of March, Harper sent Freund to Cambridge to complete negotiations on this and other matters of cooperation between Harvard and Chicago, and there Freund came face-to-face with

88. Freund to Harper, December 3, 1901, Presidents' Papers 1889–1925, box 34, folder 17; also see Storr, *Harper's University*, 292; and Ellsworth, *Law on the Midway*, 57–58.

89. Ernst Freund, "Introduction of the Convocation Orator," *University* [of Chicago] *Record*, 9 (1904): 41.

90. Ibid.

91. Beale to Harper, March 17, 1902, Presidents' Papers 1889–1925, box 19, folder 5.

Ames for the first time and informed him fully of his plans for the curriculum and teaching methods of the new school.[92]

Until they met Freund, Ames and Beale apparently had been regarding Chicago as just another opportunity for the missionary zeal of a case-method teacher to work an assault along the lines of Keener's efforts at Columbia and Wigmore's at Northwestern.[93] The Chicago people no doubt had their own ideas about legal education, but once Beale arrived on the scene he would set them straight. The interview with Freund, however, evoked an extraordinary reaction. Ames and Beale immediately wrote to Harper insisting that assurances had to be given in advance that the Chicago Law School would be organized strictly on the Harvard plan. After meeting Freund, Ames and Beale must have realized for the first time that he did not represent the kind of approach to legal education that had fallen so easily to the assaults of Harvard's missionaries at institutions like Northwestern. There was no guarantee that Beale could carry the day against Freund at Chicago. Consequently, the best course seemed to be for Ames to appeal to President Harper's sense of educational fashion and resolve matters before Beale got to Chicago:

> I understand it to be your wish and purpose to establish at your University a law-school resembling as closely as possible in its curriculum, methods of study, and quality of its Faculty, the Harvard Law School. Do not understand me as believing now that this is not still your wish and purpose. But knowing your high estimate of Professor Freund, and having discovered how widely his conception of your new School differs in fundamentals from our School, I feel that before further steps are taken we ought to clear away all possibility of any subsequent misunderstanding and disappointment.[94]

92. Harper to Freund, March 26, 1902, Presidents' Papers 1889–1925, box 34, folder 17; for the Harper-Harvard negotiations, see Ellsworth, *Law on the Midway*, 62–65, 68; and Storr, *Harper's University*, 294.

93. Compare Beale's letters to Harper of March 17, 1902, and March 27, 1902, which are all sweetness and light, with that of April 2, 1902, which definitely is not; Presidents' Papers 1889–1925, box 19, folder 5.

94. Ames to Harper, March 31, 1902, ibid.; also see Storr, *Harper's University*, 293; Williston, *Life and Law*, 206; and Ellsworth, *Law on the Midway*, 68–73.

Ames' letter to Harper has been regarded by some observers as almost an ultimatum by the dean of the nation's preeminent law school.[95] But considering Stone's observation about Chicago's importance to the triumph of the case method, it seems more likely that the letter was something of a bluff by a man who, knowing the rationalizations that underlay the case method, was apprehensive that the advance of the Harvard system might be checked at the eleventh hour. Ames informed Harper:

> Our School is conspicuous for its belief in the learning of law by the systematic study of Cases. If Professor Beale is to be Dean . . . he must have a Faculty that believes in that method. . . . Certainly [Freund's] belief in the general methods of the German Universities, and his general views as to the function of a law-school would predispose him against a thorough-going belief in us or our methods. . . . I cannot think it wise, therefore, that Professor Beale should subject our School to the loss of his teaching, until he is assured that he is to have a body of colleagues who will support him loyally because of their belief in him and his methods.[96]

Ames went on to insist upon "a curriculum of pure law" as an additional price of Beale's coming, and then closed with sentiments that were not quite genuine:

> Should you decide not to invite Mr. Beale after reading this letter . . . I need hardly say, that we shall be quite content. Nor shall we lose our interest in your School. On the contrary, we shall watch its development under favorable auspices, upon lines different from ours, with the hope that it may not only achieve a distinct success, but that it may throw new light upon the problem of legal education.

Ames' true feelings, as Beale informed Freund in a letter a few days later, was that he had been "disturbed . . . by what he (and I) consider your heretical ideas about law. The hard fight which he and Mr. Langdell had . . . made him anxious that I should not meet a similar difficulty." Beale went on to

95. Stevens, "Two Cheers for 1870," p. 438, n. 56; comment, "Ernst Freund," 763.

96. Ames to Harper, March 31, 1902, Presidents' Papers 1889–1925, box 19, folder 5.

assure Freund that "we could get on charmingly. . . . you are a lawyer and have taught law, and it is therefore a matter of course that you shall have your share in the formation of the school's policy."[97] But Beale never intended to keep this promise, for his own letter to Harper had surpassed Ames' in its demands:

> We should have assumed that everybody in Chicago was of the same mind [about Harvard methods], if it had not been for the ideas of Mr. Freund expressed here. . . . what he had in mind was absolutely opposed to our ideas and methods. I could be of no use in such a school. . . .
>
> We take a student for three years, and demand all of his time. We permit him to do no serious work outside the strictly legal subjects we teach. . . . The faculty . . . is composed solely of persons who teach *law* in the strict sense of the word.[98]

Beale went on to suggest to Harper that Freund's ideas would only reproduce at Chicago the plan of the Columbia Law School. "The curriculum of that school also includes a few non-legal electives from the School of Political Science. These facts have been suggested as accountable for the striking failure of the school to take the position to which her location, her wealth, and the ability of her faculty seem to entitle her."[99]

Such an argument could not have been lost on an institution-builder like Harper, and Beale suggested that "it is obviously necessary to choose one conception of the school or the other." Beale insisted on "distinct and definite assurances" from Harper that Chicago would adopt the Harvard plan completely, including an agreement that "no person shall teach in the school who does not frankly concur in adopting for the school the spirit and the methods of the Harvard Law School."[100] There is no record that these were ever given, and Beale ultimately was to fail in his clear intention of excluding

97. Beale to Freund, April 7, 1902, quoted in part in Storr, *Harper's University*, 295.

98. Beale to Harper, April 2, 1902, Presidents' Papers 1889–1925, box 19, folder 5.

99. Ibid.

100. Ibid.

Freund from the Chicago law faculty. But beyond having to live with Freund, he was to get his way in practically every other respect. By May, 1902, Freund was eliminated as a force at the Law School, and it was established that all instruction would be "entirely by the case method."[101] Freund was placed on faculty committees for correspondence and publicity, and several others of no particular consequence. And he was carefully excluded from the committees that determined curriculum or recommended faculty appointments.[102]

Thus, Freund, who had been working for the establishment of the Law School since 1895 and who only several months before had thought of himself as the author of its fundamental policies, found himself occupied with such duties as ordering books for the library.[103] But when Beale moved to give the young Harvard graduates that he had recruited a faculty rank

101. Law School Faculty Minutes, 1902–27, item 1 (n.d.), p. 3, University of Chicago Library.

102. For Freund's loss of influence, see ibid., and minutes of April 15, 16, 1902, November 7, 1902, February 5, 1903, April 4, 1903. (At the last meeting, the curriculum committee was expanded to include "all professors doing full work in the Law School." This still excluded Freund since he held a joint appointment.) Also see Storr, *Harper's University*, 295.

Ellsworth in *Law on the Midway* maintains that Freund retained substantial influence, but I do not see the basis for such a conclusion either in his evidence or in mine (see chap. 2, sec. 2, below). Moreover, he describes Chicago under Beale as a departure from the Harvard "pure law" model, apparently on the basis of a misapprehension of Harvard practice. In fact, most of the practices that he describes as departures could be found at Harvard. As early as 1885, the Law School's entry in *The Harvard University Catalogue* advised law students that they could cross-register in the College and that courses in "Roman Law, Political Economy, and History, are particularly suitable for Law Students" (see entry for 1884–85). In the Law School itself, courses were offered in legal history (beginning with the entry for 1887–88), statutes (beginning with the entry for 1897–98, although it is not clear whether the course was ever actually given), comparative jurisprudence (beginning with the entry for 1898–99), and administrative law (beginning with the entry for 1900–1901). The last was an optional lecture course, and its meaning will be discussed in chap. 2, below. Why such offerings did not dilute the purity of the Harvard model will be discussed at chap. 2, sec. 2, below. For Ellsworth's differing views, see *Law on the Midway*, 71–110.

103. Freund to Harper, July 20, 1902, Presidents' Papers 1889–1925, box 19, folder 5.

and compensation greater than Freund's, Freund finally protested. In a letter to Harper at the end of May, he complained that "you agreed with me two weeks ago when I said that it was to me an essential point that I should be assured of being placed upon a footing of equality with the other men, but you are now unable to make any definite assurance. . . . I think I should not be expected to bind myself to join the school permanently upon terms which will place me in a position of inferiority to younger men." He proposed to return to the political science department, and as at Columbia, let law students take his courses on an optional basis. "The plan is not what I have hoped for, but . . . it presents an escape from a situation which two days ago seemed to me intolerable."[104]

So confronted, Beale and Harper agreed to a compromise under which Freund would hold a joint appointment in law and political science. He would teach some courses that both law students and nonlaw students could take, and other courses that were to be given exclusively at the Law School or in the political science department.[105] Freund thus embarked upon a teaching career of thirty years in an institutional framework that was only slightly improved over Columbia's from the standpoint of administrative law. He would struggle to the end of his life to produce a novel scholarship in an environment that was hostile to it, both at Chicago and in the larger world of legal education. And even in these circumstances, he would almost succeed.[106]

But the immediate future now belonged to Harvard. Whatever contribution legal scholarship would make to the evolution of American administrative government over the next decade would now come out of a law school environment where the preservation of the case method was always the operative motive. With the fall of Chicago into line, the Har-

104. Freund to Harper, May 20, 1902, Presidents' Papers 1889–1925, box 34, folder 17.

105. Beale to Harper, February 14, 1904, Presidents' Papers 1889–1925, box 19, folder 6; University of Chicago *Annual Register* for 1902–3 through 1914–15 (Law School and Department of Political Science).

106. See chap. 3, sec. 3, and chap. 4, sec. 2, below.

vard model of legal education continued to spread rapidly throughout the country, and in 1903, Ames declared victory for the case method and suggested that the time for a close scrutiny of its relative merits had passed: "I do not wish to engage in any discussion on the merits of the case system of teaching. You remember the remark of the court to counsel who was arguing very strenuously on one occasion, 'Why do you labor so? The court is with you.' Now I feel that way in regard to the case system. The battle is fought."[107]

107. Ames, "Discussion of President's Address," 662.

2

The Foundations of Understanding, 1902–13

1

Even before the suppression of Ernst Freund at Chicago, Harvard's view of administrative decision-making had begun to evolve. Whereas Freund, like Goodnow, approached the administrative process on its own terms, as a problem suggesting no particular result before it was researched and reasoned through, the Harvard approach was in many respects a scholarship of avoidance. It was determined to argue away findings that might imply that the routine and responsibilities of the courts needed to be modified with regard to administration. This was not an illegitimate approach. To respond to new challenges in law with a near absolute predisposition in favor of the routine and structure of the traditional order is an approach that can be appreciated with some sympathy, and it is one that has many antecedents in Anglo-American legal development. But it is also one that in its absoluteness does not belong in spirit to the modern university. While the scholarship of the early twentieth-century university, particularly in the social sciences, has come to be seen as heavily value-laden, its open-endedness in comparison with the scholarship of the law schools is still striking; and while case-method teachers strenuously maintained that the law school belonged in the university, this difference was not one of degree only.[1]

The beginning of the Harvard approach was a series of lectures on administrative law given between 1900 and 1903 by

1. Merle Curti, ed., *American Scholarship in the Twentieth Century* (Cambridge: Harvard University Press, 1953), 15–16, 43–44.

Bruce Wyman, a young professor at the Law School. The subject thus appeared at Harvard before it did at most other schools, although it was not to be a credit course until the 1940s. Since Wyman's lectures were not given by the case method, they were optional and did not count toward the LL.B. Although Wyman is little known today, his treatment of administrative decision-making—indeed, his basic scheme for all of administrative law, which he published in treatise form in 1903[2]—was to be followed with little modification almost to the present.

Wyman's scheme envisioned an administrative law that was concerned with practically every aspect of governmental administration. But this did not mean that the attention of judges and legal scholars was to penetrate as deeply into the workings of administration as this law did. For upon closer examination, Wyman shows us that "administrative law" is to be conceived of as having two quite different components: an "internal" administrative law, and an "external" administrative law. While both may be thought of as "law" for the sake of placing their concerns within the legal order, only the latter has those attributes which make it "law" in the sense that it is fit to be treated by judges and legal scholars, or to be taught in law schools.[3] Wyman's internal-external terminology has fallen into disuse, but the division of attention that it describes has been adhered to throughout this century.

According to Wyman, the internal law concerns the formulation of specific policies by the administration and the wisdom of its decisions in cases where those policies are applied. The "internal law . . . is from first to last an unfixed obligation, one way in one case, another in another, as expediency dictates." It is that part of administrative law which "governs the processes by which the laws in general [i.e., statutes] are carried into execution by the officers of the administration," and

2. Bruce Wyman, *Principles of Administrative Law* (St. Paul, Minn.: Keefe-Davidson, 1903); also see the Law School's entry in *The Harvard University Catalogue* for 1900–1901 under "Extra Courses."

3. Wyman, *Administrative Law*, 4, 11.

because it is an "unfixed obligation," it is not the meat of courts or scholars or law schools.[4]

The external law, on the other hand, is. This is the law that "governs the *jurisdiction* of the administration over controversies that arise in the course of the execution of the [statutory] law."[5] It does not concern the substantive policies and decision-making of the administration, but rather "the relations of the administration, and of officials, with citizens."[6] These relations are obligations that were fixed by the legislature when it created the administration and gave it warrant to deal with certain classes of problems in a certain manner; and because they are fixed obligations, they may be reviewed by the courts.

In treating the external law, the "question before the judiciary is whether there has been legal administration or illegal administration, never whether there has been proper administration or improper administration." The question is whether the administration acted within the jurisdiction laid out for it by the legislature, and not the propriety of its actions within that jurisdiction. Thus, "all action by an officer in pursuance of [the statutory] law is legal; . . . all official action in pursuance of discretion vested in the officer by law is action in accordance with [law] in whatever way that discretion may be exercised. In such action an officer cannot be in the position of a wrong-doer whatever it may be."[7]

Thus, as long as the administration acts within the jurisdiction created for it by the legislature, its policies and decisions are final. "Although the judiciary may well entertain issues involving external administrative law [i.e., jurisdiction], all questions involving internal administrative law [i.e., policy] should be decided upon by the administration itself, free from the review of any other department." The substance of the administration's policy-making may be conceived of as falling within the legal order, but it is not a matter for the close scru-

4. Ibid., 13–14; also see p. 20.
5. Ibid., 342 (emphasis added).
6. Ibid., 9.
7. Ibid., 20, 11.

tiny of courts or legal scholars. "Without doubt this rule is of great consequence; it is, indeed, at the foundation of administrative law in a country subject to the common law system."[8]

If this were the whole of the proposition, there would be no need to mention Wyman, or to speak of a distinctive Harvard approach to administration. For what has been set forth is little more than the law of officers as evolved by the courts during the nineteenth century. Before the rise of a recognizable administrative process at the end of that century, these officers were unmistakably located in the executive branch of government and possessed little discretion in enforcing what were usually detailed legislative enactments. With a few notable exceptions, such as the Land Office, administrative officers enforced a statute not by adjudication, but by executing its explicit terms. If a citizen who was affected by these terms did not want to complain in a court of law about the lawfulness of the statute itself, he had to content himself with alleging that the officers who had executed it had acted beyond their jurisdiction as defined in the statute—for example, that a sheriff and/or health officers had destroyed a diseased animal instead of imposing the quarantine provided for by statute. Administrators did not do judicial work, and consequently there was nothing in the substance of an administrative decision for the courts to review, unless they wished to infringe upon the functions of another branch of government.[9]

However, with the rise of the administrative process, enabling legislation became less explicit, and defining its substantive meaning became caught up with a process of adjudication by administrators. By 1900, the courts had tentatively extended the old doctrines of the law of officers to this new and essentially different phenomenon. This extension had begun before the degree to which the administrative process would involve adjudication was apparent, and by 1900 the

8. Ibid., 328, 85, 11.

9. J. Forrester Davison and Nathan D. Grundstein, *Administrative Law and the Regulatory System*, rev. ed. (Washington: Lerner Law Book Co., 1968), 5–6.

case law was by no means settled as to whether the extension had been appropriate. Wyman sought to show that it had been.[10]

The distinguishing characteristic of American administrative law—that the decisions of administrators within the scope of their authority are final—can be traced back to the influence of Wyman's work. Although the form of the treatise is simply that of a restatement of the case law of the courts in succinct and coordinated fashion, it must be remembered that the coordination of cases for a Langdellian scholar was a process of distinguishing the "good" cases from the bad. The judges in their daily routine were presumed to be unable to see the forest for the trees, and it remained for the scholar by the force of superior analysis to demonstrate that the mass of cases suggested a particular solution, "if only we have the insight to realize it."[11] Wyman meant to show why an administration possessing the judicial power could still be treated by the courts like the administration of the mid-nineteenth century. Given the nature of the modern administrative process, Wyman's treatise, though it seemed only to restate the case law, was in fact a work of creative scholarship.[12]

Indeed, the most creative element in Wyman's treatise did not concern cases at all, although it was used to support his view of the cases. This was Wyman's omission of any reference to Goodnow's *Comparative Administrative Law*. Goodnow had discussed the implications of French practice for American administrative adjudication. But Wyman maintained that

10. Wyman, *Administrative Law*, 85–98; John Dickinson, *Administrative Justice and the Supremacy of Law in the United States* (Cambridge: Harvard University Press, 1927), 41ff.

11. Bruce Wyman, *Control of the Market* (New York: Moffat, Yard, 1911), 277; this work is the best source for the jurisprudential assumptions of Wyman's scholarship, and, as will be seen, these assumptions did not change between 1903 and 1911; also see ibid., 275; and Bruce Wyman, "State Control of Public Utilities," *Harvard Law Review*, 24 (1911): 624–31.

12. Wyman, *Administrative Law*, 327–28; Thomas Reed Powell, "Administrative Exercise of the Police Power," *Harvard Law Review*, 24 (1911): 268–89, 333–46, 441–59; Dickinson, *Administrative Justice*, 41ff. I credit Dickinson with first fully recognizing Wyman's "creativity."

"so new is this function in the administration to try its own controversies that no discussion of it is to be found in our law writers."[13] Wyman was able to ignore Goodnow's treatise because it had the appearance of not being a work of legal scholarship, coming as it did from a faculty of political science. Goodnow's later scholarship in fact dealt heavily with political science—his landmark *Politics and Administration* appeared in 1900—and this served to strengthen the impression that *Comparative Administrative Law* belonged to political science also.[14]

Instead of addressing Goodnow's findings, Wyman dismissed the entire French experience by means of a brief reference to Albert Dicey's famous analysis of the *droit administratif*. According to Dicey, the French system was utterly opposed to Anglo-American conceptions of the rule of law, for "servants of the state are in their official capacity to a great extent protected from the ordinary law of the land, exempted from the jurisdiction of the ordinary tribunals, and subject to official law administered by official bodies."[15] "Official law" was whatever suited the whim of an oppressive state. Dicey, who was Vinerian professor of English law at Oxford, had originally published his account of French administrative law in 1885 as part of his imposing *Lectures Introductory to the Study of the Law of the Constitution*. By 1900, this work had come to be regarded as a classic. But with the sixth edition, appearing in 1902, Dicey recanted his earlier view of the French system, saying that it had been a misconception based upon his reading of outdated French sources. It is unclear whether Wyman was unaware of Dicey's sixth edition, or chose not to acknowledge it.[16]

In any event, nine years earlier Goodnow had accurately

13. Wyman, *Administrative Law*, 321.

14. See pp. 48–49, above.

15. Wyman, *Administrative Law*, 2.

16. Wyman did not cite an edition; for Dicey's contacts with Harvard, see Richard A. Cosgrove, "A. V. Dicey at the Harvard Law School, 1898: A Study in Anglo-American Legal Community," *Harvard Library Bulletin*, 26 (1978): 325–35; for Dicey's change of view, see James W. Garner, "Anglo-

portrayed the contemporary state of French administrative jurisprudence, relying on the latest French authors including Laferrière, the intellectual founder of the modern *droit administratif*. Thus, Wyman's reliance on Dicey's original account seems rather dubious. Goodnow showed that the intensive review of the justiciable controversies of the administration by French administrative courts had provided the latter with a specialized jurisprudence for vindicating the rights of citizens affected by administrative action. In addition, this review had yielded an understanding of the needs of the administration as a policy-making instrument of the state. According to Goodnow, the French administrative courts were better equipped than the courts of common law countries to arrive at decisions upon review that preserved both private right and administrative efficiency. Prodded by intensive review, the process of administrative adjudication had resulted in an articulate experience with the problems of administrative government, serving to make more explicit the terms of enabling statutes or to point up the unattainable quality of their assumptions and expectations. As a lesson of French practice, however, Goodnow did not recommend the severe segregation of the administrative courts from the regular courts that prevailed in France. This was a consequence of attitudes toward the regular courts arising from the Revolution. For the United States, Goodnow only suggested the possibility of creating lower appellate courts of specialized jurisdiction within the prevailing judicial systems of the states and the federal government.[17]

Wyman, of course, did not address these perspectives. It is difficult to decide, in assessing his scholarship, whether Wyman ignored the evidence of *Comparative Administrative*

American and Continental European Administrative Law," *New York University Law Quarterly Review*, 7 (1929): 387–88.

17. Frank J. Goodnow, *Comparative Administrative Law* (New York: Putnam, 1893), 12–14, 144–46, 217–25, 303–7; also see Nathan D. Grundstein, "Presidential Power, Administration, and Administrative Law; Part I: The Theoretical Beginnings," *George Washington Law Review*, 18 (1950): 321–23.

Law, or whether the canons of case-method scholarship simply did not require him to read it in the first place. But a hint is provided by Williston, who tells us that "the library of the Harvard Law School owes its extensive collection of treatises . . . of the modern civil law" to Ames' "habit when puzzled by a question of theoretical jurisprudence to see if light could be obtained from the writings of continental lawyers."[18] Williston himself would "study some troublesome questions of contract law in the writers of France and Germany."[19] Yet this willingness to go outside of the common law was not all that it seemed to be. "I had no desire to make a thorough study of any foreign legal system, but only to obtain suggestions of principles that might be applicable to Anglo-American law."[20] Thus, a case-method scholar's reading in a foreign system could be highly selective; and given the degree of his partiality for the common law, any evidence from the foreign system that suggested a need for substantial modifications in American law, and consequently in the routines of the law schools, was not construed as a suggestion at all. This filtering process was nothing more than the classic response of the common-law lawyer to foreign systems. But the Harvard Law School men claimed to be something more: scholars of the modern university.[21]

If, as French practice implied, the substance of American administrative adjudication was suitable for judicial review, the institutional structure of the courts would have to be substantially modified to accommodate such review; their jurisprudence would come to be increasingly concerned with, and perhaps dominated by, issues of industrial and social regulation arising out of administrative controversies; and the law school would experience something like a revolution in its curriculum and its scholarship. Therefore, the only acceptable

18. Samuel Williston, "James Barr Ames—His Services to Legal Education," *Harvard Law Review*, 23 (1910): 331.

19. Samuel Williston, *Life and Law* (Boston: Little, Brown, 1940), 258.

20. Ibid., 259.

21. See p. 40, above.

conclusion for a man of Wyman's loyalties had to be that the substance of administrative adjudication was not reviewable, that the administrator's decision was final within the scope of his authority.

It was one thing for the judges to have tentatively arrived at this result in the case law. Being in government, they had, and needed to have, a strong sense of institutional identity and self-preservation. Their initial response to the rising administrative process was reasonable and to be expected. But it was quite another thing, given the claims of the Harvard Law School about its works, for Wyman to purport as a scholar to find that this result inhered analytically in the nature of administrative adjudication. "In all adjudication by the administration upon close examination there are signs of the administrative nature of the proceedings," he says. "Things are done in administrative adjudication which could never be done in the judicial process."[22] But Wyman cannot present the evidence to support his claim, and he relies instead upon constantly repeating it. Nowhere can he show that the issues which are presented for administrative adjudication are substantially different in their justiciable character from those which the courts decide. His signs of administrative difference reduce themselves to inconsequential ones in procedure, and to a description of the nature of the administrative power to decide controversies which cannot be differentiated from the judicial power.

The foundation of administrative adjudication, Wyman tells us, is the discretion of the decider. Unlike judges, administrators may decide "as expediency dictates." At best, it is "rules for the ordinary case, free of these rules in the extraordinary case."[23] But a sense of an analogous judicial discretion had been arrived at by legal scholars in 1900, although not by the legal profession as a whole. For example, there are striking similarities between Ezra Ripley Thayer's understanding of

22. Wyman, *Administrative Law*, 341.
23. Ibid., 13, 333.

the judicial function in his article "Judicial Legislation" (1891) and Wyman's description of administrative adjudication.[24] Indeed, the bulk of Wyman's discussion of administrative adjudication does not go to showing that it is something different, but to giving reasons why the location of this power within the administration need not be conceptually troublesome.

In this respect, the ultimate palliative is judicial review. In Wyman's scheme, judicial review is not supposed to go to the substance of an administrative decision, but under "our system the courts in the last resort may inquire into . . . the validity of administration."[25] In the event of a gross injustice, the administrative decision will be reached and voided by a reviewing court under the pretext that the administration has violated some procedural requirement in arriving at its decision. This device must be used sparingly, but its availability helps to lessen the lawyer's interest in what it is conceptually that the administration does.[26]

This interest may be further dulled by realizing that expertise, that elixir of the administration, is present in its adjudication, ensuring that bad substantive decisions will be rare, and in any case discouraging unexpert judges from reviewing too often the substantive results. It is difficult to tell from Wyman's discussion what exactly expertise consists of, and how it is different from the knowledge which judges acquire in the course of their duties. But Wyman suggests that lawyers as-

24. Ezra R. Thayer, "Judicial Legislation: Its Legitimate Function in the Development of the Common Law," *Harvard Law Review*, 5 (1891): 172–201.

25. Wyman, *Administrative Law*, 67.

26. By way of contrast, in continental Europe the regular courts by 1800 had lost a control they once possessed over the administration, with the result that the legal profession was not distracted by an imagined judicial supremacy from developing the parts of the administrative process that were suited to judicial methods. See C. J. Friedrich, "The Continental Tradition of Training Administrators in Law and Jurisprudence," *Journal of Modern History*, 11 (1939): 139; and Reginald Parker, "The Historic Basis of Administrative Law: Separation of Powers and Judicial Supremacy," *Rutgers Law Review*, 12 (1958): 464–65, 476–81.

sume its existence and not worry about the substance of administrative decision-making.[27]

Having prepared his readers in this way, Wyman was ready to make them understand why the familiar rule of the separation of powers did not apply to the adjudication of the administration. If this doctrine had been rigidly enforced, the growth of the administrative process into its present institutional form would have been impossible, and consequently we are inclined today to regard the separation of powers as a quaint abstraction. But to the lawyers of 1900 it still seemed to be an imposing requirement of constitutional jurisprudence. If it did not absolutely prohibit adjudication by the administration, it at least suggested that the substantive results must be reviewed by courts of law.[28] Wyman, however, countered this thrust with a subsidiary doctrine of incidental powers: "What may be provided is some co-operation between the departments—the lending to the administration of the process of the courts. This, it is suggested, is the solution of this problem in accordance with constitutional law under our system of government with its three departments—independence with inter-relation."[29] This, like almost every other argument in Wyman's treatise, may be traced back to the case law of the nineteenth-century courts. But the point which he gave to it was creative in the fullest sense of the word.[30]

Thus, the availability of a judicial review that might occasionally glance at substance, the idea of administrative expertise, and the doctrine of incidental powers were all useful devices of avoidance. Yet another device was proceduralism. In time this was to become the major prop of an American administrative law that sought to control the administrative process while skirting its substance—although with Wyman it

27. Wyman, *Administrative Law*, 85.

28. See, for instance, Cuthbert W. Pound, "The Judicial Power," *Harvard Law Review*, 35 (1922): 787–96.

29. Wyman, *Administrative Law*, 97.

30. Ibid., 85–98; also see Robert E. Cushman, *The Independent Regulatory Commissions* (New York: Oxford University Press, 1941), 421–27.

still appears as a lesser aid to avoidance. After 1920, the "external law" (in Wyman's terminology) came to be concerned not only with the administrator's scope of authority as defined in enabling legislation, but also, and in great detail, with the procedures by which administrators reached decisions.[31] Wyman seems to have been aware of the potential of this element in the external law without dwelling on it. He clearly saw how close proceduralism can come to the substantive control of the administrative process without committing the courts to substantive review in an explicit or systematic manner. For instance, Wyman suggests that it would be a violation of (procedural) due process if the administration's discretion to decide controversies were so free that it amounted to mere caprice; and he suggests that administrative discretion would be capricious if it ignored entirely the logical force of the administration's prior pronouncements (in case opinions or in administrative regulations) on a given issue. Thus, a reviewing court may occasionally examine administrative substance, but supposedly it is only to effect a procedural standard.[32] Like the other devices of Wyman's approach, proceduralism seemed to permit a judicial control of the administrative process by the backdoor.

2

In his endeavor to show that "our common law, by which we are so largely governed, may be relied upon to meet . . . the complex conditions created by . . . industrial organization,"[33] Wyman was supported by a senior colleague at the Harvard Law School: Joseph Beale, who from 1902 to 1904 was also serving as the dean of the new University of Chicago Law School. Beale had taught the law of common carriers and public service companies before Wyman's arrival at Harvard, and

31. Davison and Grundstein, *Administrative Law*, 7–8.
32. Wyman, *Administrative Law*, 254–55, 303, 333.
33. Wyman, *Control of the Market*, 1.

in 1906 the two men would coauthor a treatise on the case law concerning the Interstate Commerce Commission.[34]

During his Chicago tenure, it could not have escaped Beale's attention that the longer Ernst Freund was hindered in fully developing his "heretical ideas about law,"[35] the more time was given to legal scholars after the Harvard fashion to develop a consensus that the substance and uses of the newer forms of governmental power need not be closely inquired into. Accordingly, Freund was given no opportunity for the testing or refinement of his ideas in his teaching.[36]

The administrative law course that Freund had intended to give during the Law School's first year of operation (1902–3) was restricted by Beale to graduate students and undergraduate seniors. Not until the following year, when Freund had worked up a course based on cases, was he permitted to offer administrative law to law students—with disastrous consequences for the progress of his scholarship.[37] The subject now had to become what it appeared to be in the cases. From the partial perspective of the regular courts that reviewed administrative action, administrative law was an exercise in appealing administrative decisions based upon nonsubstantive errors by administrative authorities. Any other concern could have little place in a course built on cases. Although it would later seem to Freund that "the failure of the [administrative] process up to the present time to produce satisfactory results . . . is due in part at least to the insufficient attention that has been given the modalities of delegation and their effects,"[38] there was little he could do to correct this as a teacher in a regime of "pure law." He had to content himself with compil-

34. *The Law of Railroad Rate Regulation* (Boston: William J. Nagel, 1906).

35. Beale to Freund, April 7, 1902, quoted in part in Richard J. Storr, *Harper's University: The Beginnings* (Chicago: University of Chicago Press, 1966), 295; see p. 55, above.

36. See p. 95, below.

37. See University of Chicago *Annual Register*, 1901–2, p. 204 (course 24) and p. 365 (following course 41); and ibid., 1902–3, p. 397 (course 67).

38. Ernst Freund, "Prolegomena to a Science of Legislation," *Illinois Law Review*, 13 (1918): 287.

ing a casebook for the course: "In compiling my collection of 'Cases on Administrative Law' I attempted to include this matter; but the results were unsatisfactory owing to the scarcity of case material."[39]

Still, informally with his students, Freund tried to suggest what he considered to be the true dimensions of his subject and its place in the legal order. But for students who had been steeped in the case method—Freund was carefully excluded from teaching in the first year—the transition to a more comprehensive outlook was very difficult. They complained about the "mental telepathy which was necessary in order to answer his questions. . . . Freund did not give himself to expounding questions of legal technique or discussing the basic interests or the difficulties involved in particular cases." Rather, he looked at the legal system as a whole, "and then tried to make some sense out of it." To the students, this inexcusable failure "to discuss the claims involved in the cases or comment upon the judicial presuppositions in handling them" was attributed to the fact that Freund must be "a continental or civil law lawyer [a pejorative term] and not particularly conscious of our Constitution."[40] Teaching, it was becoming clear, was not going to reinforce scholarship, and Freund soon fell into line and pretended that "as regards methods of instruction, there was little hesitation in adopting the so-called 'case method'" in the spring of 1902.[41]

Beale naturally was delighted that Freund offered so little opposition, and the dean simply ceased to regard him as a factor at the Law School.[42] By the spring of 1904, when he

39. Ibid.

40. Paul L. Sayre, "A Common Law of Administrative Powers," *Iowa Law Review*, 18 (1933): 242–43.

41. "The University of Chicago Law School," *University* [of Chicago] *Record*, 12 (1908): 100; for evidence of Freund's authorship, or contributing authorship, see p. 103.

42. Beale to William Rainey Harper, April 2, 1903, Presidents' Papers 1889–1925, box 19, folder 5, University of Chicago Library ("With a faculty composed of Wigmore, Mack, Mechem, Whittier and a bright young man, even supposing Hall to come to Cambridge, I should feel that I left in Chicago the strongest law faculty in the country, on the average"). While Beale

was preparing to return to Cambridge, Beale was highly satisfied with the events of the past two years, a period in which Wyman had come to flower while Freund lay fallow. The dean described his feelings to a commencement audience in June: "The spirit in which professional study must be carried on is the same as the spirit of all scholarship—to know the truth and to extend its borders." This, according to Beale, was the spirit which animated the law schools of Harvard and Chicago. "If so carried on," he continued, "professional instruction is profoundly liberalizing." Indeed, it "must be taught principally by men who have devoted their lives to investigating the truth, and to training others in its ways."[43]

Apparently Freund, who introduced Beale on this occasion, was mistaken about the state of affairs in law schools. Was he, as his students liked to say, really a civil lawyer who misperceived the American system and ignored its Constitution? According to Freund, the law teacher could "not in his class press the inquiring spirit too far. He is in a very different position from a teacher of medicine where the relentless pursuit of truth can never be an obstacle to professional training."[44] Freund apparently did not understand, as Beale did, that law at Chicago was being taught "as all sciences are taught—by touching the imagination, by filling the heart, and by re-creating the mind." Surely, "it must be clear that such a science studied in the university must be studied in university fashion."[45]

Interestingly, when Beale was not required to address a general university audience, but one made up of his fellow case-method teachers, his opinions on the value and necessity of a university approach in teaching law changed considerably.

---

made an occasional reference to Freund in his correspondence with Harper, more typically Freund was absent from Beale's discussions of substantial Law School matters, such as the item quoted.

43. Joseph H. Beale, Jr., "The Place of Professional Education in the Universities," *University* [of Chicago] *Record*, 9 (1904): 44, 46.

44. Ernst Freund, "Law School and University," *University* [of Chicago] *Record*, 18 (1932): 150; Freund was reviewing the history of the Law School.

45. Beale, "The Place of Professional Education," 46.

Then the case drills of the Harvard Law School classroom assumed supreme importance. Anything else was extraneous, except perhaps in the first week of the academic year. That was the week at the Law School "before the students have been assigned their seats, before we have in front of us the chart that tells us the names, and before, therefore, we can call on the students to take their part in the discussion." The case drill lost its appeal if the professors could not call on a student by name for interrogation. So in the first week, there seemed to be nothing better to do than to give the students "some talk about what the law is . . . and some little rearrangement of legal ideas. . . . They take it down in their notebooks . . . and from time to time later they take comfort in it."[46] But the real sense of what the law was would come to the students "in the course of the first year's instruction," with their total absorption in the particular issues of particular cases, and "before the beginning of the second year they are lawyers" in the Harvard fashion, immunized against the occasional crank course of a "continental lawyer" teaching administrative law.[47]

Those quite different sentiments which Beale had expressed on commencement day in Chicago in 1904 had their uses, however, and in fact belonged quite legitimately to the Harvard Law School tradition. They were Langdell's thoughts at the time of his coming to Harvard, when he had been confident of building a knowledge-oriented science of law. Beale had even told his Chicago audience that "the library is the laboratory of our science,"[48] and although such phrases had for almost two decades lost their original meaning, they still served as an effective advertisement for the case method. A general university audience could be counted on to take them at face value, and the occasional individual like Freund who did not could be brought into line by other means.

46. Remarks of J. H. Beale, "Papers and Discussion Concerning the Redlich Report," *American Law School Review*, 4 (1916): 107.

47. Ibid.; Sayre, "Administrative Powers," 243.

48. Beale, "The Place of Professional Education," 46; compare the remarks of Langdell at p. 29, above.

Thus, the borders of truth were extended, and in the spring of 1904 Joseph Beale returned to Cambridge, filled with a sense of achievement.

3

In only a year's time, however, events began to unfold that severely tested the Harvard view of administrative decision-making and its relation to the courts. The creation of a powerful railroad commission in Wisconsin in 1905 began a tremendous expansion of administrative government during the Progressive Era. With the discovery of the administrative commission as a supposedly ideal instrument of government, enabling legislation became increasingly indefinite, and consequently administrators resorted more and more to adjudication as a means of making some sense out of the industrial world they were to regulate—a development with threatening implications for Wyman's scheme of keeping the substantive concerns of administration at arm's length from the courts.[49]

The administrative experience with the greatest potential for collapsing Wyman's scheme was to be New York's. The New York Public Service Commissions were created in 1907 under the leadership of governor Charles Evans Hughes. According to Herbert Croly in *The Promise of American Life*, the "most complete existing type of [administrative] . . . power is not the Federal Interstate Commerce Commisssion, but the Public Service Commissions of New York State."[50] In particular, Hughes had led a fight against intensive judicial

49. See Introduction, sec. 2, above; for the Wisconsin commission, see Stanley P. Caine, *The Myth of a Progressive Reform: Railroad Regulation in Wisconsin, 1903–1910* (Madison: State Historical Society of Wisconsin, 1970).

50. Herbert Croly, *The Promise of American Life* (New York: Macmillan, 1909), 360; for another estimate of the importance of the New York commissions, see Delos F. Wilcox, "Effects of State Regulation upon the Municipal Ownership Movement," American Academy of Political and Social Science, *Annals*, 53 (1914): 71.

review of the Commissions' decision-making, using Wyman's arguments in defense of his position.[51]

However, almost immediately after their creation, one of the Commissions—the Second District Commission, which supervised the entire state outside of New York City—began to employ fully developed judicial methods in a significant part of its decision-making. The Commission's first chairman was a little-known lawyer named Frank W. Stevens, who soon perceived that ideas about expertise were not particularly helpful in the day-to-day reality of administrative government, and who therefore fell back on the values and approaches of his profession to the extent that it seemed practical. The legislature had empowered the Commission to regulate six major fields of business activity by public service companies: right of entry into business, capitalization, transfer of holdings and ownership, quality of service, rates, and the establishment and alteration of grade crossings. And under Stevens between 1907 and 1913, the Commission built up a case law in the first three fields. To the extent that justiciable controversies presented themselves in the field of service, a case law arose there also. The fields of rates and grade crossings were largely unsuited to this development.[52] New Yorkers did not protest this turn of events, for they simply assumed that the Commission's performance was somehow related to its "expertise."[53]

51. See Charles Evans Hughes, *Addresses and Papers* (New York: Putnam, 1908), 107. Hughes tells us in his autobiographical notes that he was a consumer of Harvard legal scholarship; see David J. Danelski and Joseph S. Tulchin, eds., *The Autobiographical Notes of Charles Evans Hughes* (Cambridge: Harvard University Press, 1973), 95.

52. See Charles S. Hyneman, "The Case Law of the New York Public Service Commission," *Columbia Law Review*, 34 (1934): 67–105; see Note on Sources: New York State, below.

53. See Harold J. Howland, "A Year of 'Government by Commission,'" *The Outlook*, 90 (1908): 483–90; Henry Bruere, "Public Utility Regulation in New York," American Academy of Political and Social Science, *Annals*, 31 (1908): 535–51; Joint Legislative Committee to Investigate Telephone and Telegraph Companies, *Report* (Albany: J. B. Lyon Company, 1910), 28–29;

Stevens did not disturb this impression. The public was taken with the idea that its commissioners were progressive "experts," not hidebound judges, and in any event it was obvious that a judicial approach could not be extended to all or even the major portion of the Commission's responsibilities. Many of these were in fact nonadjudicatory. They involved the inspection and general supervision of the business operations and trade practices of regulated companies. Moreover, many of the issues that did come to a hearing were not truly justiciable. They required the Commission to act more like a planning board than a court and could involve, for example, a decision as to the precise location, size, and kinds of accommodations for a proposed railway station.[54]

In the language of the enabling statute, this last task might seem straightforward enough. It was simply to ensure "adequate" service and accommodation. But at hearings of this sort, Stevens and his fellow commissioners found themselves entangled with the subjective preferences of the townspeople who wanted to use the station. "Whenever we endeavor to accede to the wishes of a considerable number of people upon any point, we are almost invariably met by this shifting of opinions . . . and just how to deal with it properly I confess I am puzzled to know."[55]

Thus, a commissioner's workday might involve purely executive tasks, or a hearing where the commission could do little more than act as a town meeting moderator. But there were also hearings where, Stevens believed, the "work of the Public Service Commission is in the nature of a court."[56] This was especially true where it seemed reasonable to suppose that fact situations would repeat themselves to some extent.

William Anderson, *The Work of Public Service Commissions* (Minneapolis: University of Minnesota, 1913), 30–33.

54. Anderson, *Public Service Commissions*, 15–30.

55. Frank W. Stevens to Watson T. Dunsmore, July 20, 1908, Correspondence Folder, case 9, roll 1, 2nd Dist. Cases, Central Files, New York State Public Service Commission (NYS PSC).

56. Remarks of F. W. Stevens, "Traffic News," *Railway Age Gazette*, 51 (1911): 258.

The conception of this sort of hearing work as fully judicial caused the commissioners to feel an obligation toward it that expertise could not duplicate. In Steven's words: "if [the Commission] may determine these matters, upon what principles or reasons is it to act? The statute does not set them forth. There is no escape from the conclusion that the Commission must itself establish them for its guidance."[57] Thus, "In cases which required the laying down of a principle not theretofore applied, the Commission . . . has given written opinions discussing fully the questions presented."[58]

One result of this approach was "the development of a consistent body of decisions"[59] amounting to a substantive administrative law. This did not mean, however, that consistency had become an inflexible requirement or an end in itself. There was no danger that the Commission's jurisprudence would rigidify after the fashion of the regular courts. The questions that came before the Commission were more novel and often more complex than those that came before the courts, and the chairman realized that to a greater degree than even Holmes' expediential judge "a public service commissioner must often ignore precedent and not be afraid to reverse himself."[60]

The felt obligation towards maximizing consistency that came from the judicial approach simply caused the commissioners to look closely at the similarities and differences of related cases and discuss "fully the questions presented."[61] Administrative precedents did not strait-jacket the Commission, but only disciplined its formulation of policy. It was a mistaken impression, the chairman believed, "that because [legal]

57. *Re* Application of the Delaware and Hudson Company, I P.S.C. 2nd D. 392, 416 (1908); I use the form of citation that was employed by the Commission in its reports of decisions.

58. New York State, Public Service Commission, Second District, *Second Annual Report* (Albany, 1909), 1:9; the chairman composed the text of these reports.

59. Ibid.

60. Remarks of F. W. Stevens, "New York's Public Service Commissions," *Electric Railway Journal*, 45 (1915): 1086.

61. Second District, *Second Annual Report*, 1:9.

questions are asked here they are raised as stumbling blocks. . . . what I am trying to bring out by various questions is the entire process of reasoning [involved]."[62]

By proceeding in this manner—by assuming that legal issues were involved in regulatory fact situations and seeking them out—the Commission was able to build up a considerable experience with the problems under its supervision. As a result, it could expedite the hearing process and attend to the administrative application of this experience. Stevens understood the extent to which the Commission's judicial component animated its other parts. The sheer number of complaints coming into the Commission would have overwhelmed a regular court, and there was as a result a tremendous pressure on the Commission staff to effect compromises and informal settlements between disputants rather than schedule hearings. Even when a dispute reached the hearing stage, commissioners often sought to induce an informal settlement in order to conserve time and lessen the burden of their caseload. But under Stevens, this process of inducing informal settlements was not random or haphazard. Because the Commission had a fully developed understanding of the uses of adjudication, incoming complaints could be analyzed as potentially justiciable or nonjusticiable. Of those matters that appeared to be justiciable, some presented trivial issues, some presented issues previously decided and enunciated in Commission opinions, and some presented novel questions of considerable consequence. The guidelines for formal or informal settlement were thus obvious.[63]

An even more important consequence of Stevens' under-

62. Remarks of Stevens, case 348, pp. 115, 307, roll 15, 2nd Dist. Minutes, Central Files, NYS PSC; for a general discussion of this point, see Philippe Nonet, *Administrative Justice* (New York: Russell Sage Foundation, 1969), 252.

63. Second District, *First Annual Report* (Albany, 1908), 1:34–35; Second District, *Second Annual Report*, 1:9–19, 34, 75–76; memorandum from Stevens to Commissioners Keep and Osborne, "In Matter of the Application of the Schagticoke Electric Company," case 30, Petition Folder, roll 1, 2nd Dist. Cases; testimony of Seymour Van Santvoord, Joint Legislative Committee to Investigate the Public Service Commissions, *Final Report* (Albany:

standing of the judicial function was in the area of the production and protection of Commission expressions of regulatory policy. A fully developed judicial approach tended to compel policy statements in the course of adjudication. But why should the losing party in a case be disposed to accept the policy that underlay the decision? Under Stevens, it was because the stated policy was made to appear as "law": the policy seemed to follow from the wording of the Commission's enabling statute as applied to the facts of the case—if only one would analyze the situation in a lawyer-like fashion.[64]

In Wyman's view of the administrative process, the enabling statute was regarded as setting forth primarily the jurisdiction of the administration; that is, the statute told an agency where it might act, but not how, and administrators possessed a wide discretion in their decision-making—limited only by the requirement that they be wise. In practice, this discretion invited protests by losing parties that decisions should have gone the other way, that they were not wise, and that they need not be obeyed. But Stevens purported to show that no such discretion existed in the Second District Commission, and that the decision in a case was not merely the decider's policy preference, but rather that decider and litigant alike were bound by statutory provision. This linkage between the Commission's policies and the fundamental written law of the administration—i.e., the enabling statute—had been built up bit by bit in the Commission's case law available in published reports of decisions. The losing party was challenged to peruse these volumes before making his fight, and thus he found himself bumped from an open-ended attack against the Commission's decision onto the narrow path of the law.[65]

Because Stevens took care to assert this technique only in

J. B. Lyon Company, 1915), 2:2069; testimony of Frank Irvine, ibid., 2:2241; testimony of Frank H. Mott, ibid., 2:1689–93.

64. Case 6, pp. 5–7, roll 1, 2nd Dist. Minutes; case 214, pp. 20–21, roll 11, ibid.

65. For instance, colloquy, case 3, p. 9, roll 1, ibid.; colloquies, case 348, pp. 115, 300, 307, 314, roll 15, ibid.; these exchanges, along with several

truly justiciable controversies, he was largely successful with it. In blunting the criticisms of losing parties in this manner, Stevens was tapping a dynamic which had always availed the regular courts and which later would be given classic expression by Thurman Arnold.

On the eve of the New Deal, Arnold observed that "commissions, composed of experts, can be violently criticized by editorial writers. But if the matter is appealed to a non-expert court, sitting on the same question and using the same criteria, it appears to be settled in the only way possible under the law." Arnold wondered "what peculiar talisman judges who sit as courts possess which gives them such advantages over judges who sit as bureaucrats." It was, apparently, a conviction in both the lay and the legal mind that there was such a thing as "law" and that it was a thing quite apart from the stuff of ordinary human affairs. Law was, of course, elucidated by the courts. No matter how many assaults upon these assumptions might be made in the name of "realism," they stood fast.[66]

"The courts represent the supremacy of 'law.' It is judges sitting as courts who guarantee us a government of laws and not of men, whereas judges sitting as bureaucrats or as executives are always trying to substitute a government of men and not of laws." Thus, if we are dissatisfied with a court's decision, "our quarrel is, then, with the law, which we must respect until it is changed, and not with the court which applied it." This dynamic "shifts criticism of the result away from the judge or the court to some body which is supposed to have the power to change the 'law.'"[67]

It was Stevens' achievement that he was able by the craftsman-like practice of the judicial function to convince many of the lawyers who appeared before him that the Second District's adjudications fell in the direction of the "court" side of

---

others, are reproduced in William Chase, "American Legal Scholarship and Administrative Law" (Ph.D. diss., Harvard University, 1978), at pp. 56–59, 62–67.

66. Thurman Arnold, "The Role of Substantive Law and Procedure in the Legal Process," *Harvard Law Review*, 45 (1932): 627, 629.

67. Ibid., 629, 627, 635.

Arnold's bureaucrat-court analysis. Lawyers who had lost a case before the Commission counseled their clients that they had lost on the law, and thus the Commission was left free to build up an administrative jurisprudence embodying regulatory policy.[68]

However, the view of the Commission as court which permitted this development was limited to the lawyers who actually practiced before the Commission, and their appearances were sporadic, for there was nothing like a public utilities bar in New York at this time. To widen an understanding of this experience required the service of legal scholarship, and this was not forthcoming. Legal scholars were committed to a different view of the place of administrative adjudication in the legal order, and Stevens' approach endured only as long as his tenure at the Second District Commission. By the end of 1913, the Commission's case law had fallen into disuse.[69]

But there was also an opportunity here, or from a Harvard Law School perspective, a danger. A decline of the Commission's performance as a result of Stevens' departure might cause public scrutiny of the Commission's internal procedures for the first time. What legal scholarship had failed to do—publicize the judicial component of the administrative process—might now be done by public investigation. Should this happen, the lessons of the Stevens years would quickly be brought to national prominence, for the New York commissions were the most reported and commented upon in the country, what with the nation's trade and journal press centered in New York City. Indeed, events in New York were to be just a part of a series of events over the next decade that seemed to have the potential for undoing all the work of the Harvard Law School men in administrative law and government.

68. See, for instance, the episodes reported in Bruce William Dearstyne, "Railroads and Railroad Regulation in New York State, 1900–1913" (Ph.D. diss., Syracuse University, 1974), 158–59.

69. Joint Legislative Committee to Investigate the Public Service Commissions, *Complete Report* (Albany: J. B. Lyon Company, 1917), esp. pp. 118–20, 246–50.

3

A Time of "Threatening Dangers," 1913–21

1

After Stevens' departure in 1913, the other New York commissioners might have carried on with his methods. But Stevens had been able to impose a judicial approach on the Commission by the force of his personality, and not because he had been able to convince his fellow commissioners that it was essential to the success of their work. Although they deferred to their chairman, the other commissioners believed that the weight of their regulatory powers was sufficient in itself to protect whatever policies they might wish to promulgate. It was clear that no administrative body had ever been endowed with such powers. According to the Commission's principal sponsor, Charles Evans Hughes, "wherever there is an abuse, the commission can put its finger on it and . . . stop it, no matter in what department of management it may be."[1] The commissioners could not see why they should subject themselves to the intellectual rigors involved in maintaining Stevens' administrative jurisprudence, or why they should subject the people of New York to the relatively slow development of regulatory policy that a judicial approach entailed. It seemed obvious that they had the power to strike quickly and completely.[2]

By dispensing with precedent, however, the later commis-

1. Charles Evans Hughes, *Addresses and Papers* (New York: Putnam, 1908), 137–38.

2. Testimony of Seymour Van Santvoord, Joint Legislative Committee to Investigate the Public Service Commissions, *Final Report* (Albany: J. B. Lyon Company, 1915), 2:2050, 2052; Osborne, *Commissioner*, dissenting, *Re* Application of the Buffalo, Rochester and Eastern Company, I P.S.C. 2nd

sioners severely impoverished their vocabulary of regulatory argument. In confronting the instant case, analogies to the dispositions of prior cases went unnoticed, and the later commissioners found it difficult to take action contrary to the desires of a party when they were unable to express in precise terms the need for such action. Their powers, though great in the abstract, had no cutting edge. Shunning legal argument, the later commissioners therefore took cover under the mantle of "expertise" and directed their attention to the "facts" of each case. In the words of a later chairman, "I do not believe that [the Commission] has taken what you would call a judicial position. The Commission has regarded itself as a fact-finding body; in other words, an organization constituted by the State for the purpose of finding facts."[3] But after the "facts," came a more difficult stage: "After it has found the facts, of course, it must come to a conclusion upon those facts. After it has found the facts, as I say, it must come to a conclusion."[4] This hesitancy about the stage of decision-making—about the actual operation of expertise—was typical of the later Commission.[5]

Thus, in less than a year after the abandonment of the Commission's case law, New Yorkers began to talk of a "crisis" in public service regulation. Stevens' departure brought to the surface a discontent with the Commission's performance that in fact had been building throughout the Stevens years. Since 1907, New Yorkers' perception of the degree to which the Commission had been successful corresponded almost exactly

---

D. 532, 623–24; Martin S. Decker, "Practical Versus Theoretical Railway Regulation," *Railway World*, 52 (1908): 366–69.

3. Testimony of William A. Prendergast, Commission on Revision of the Public Service Commissions Law, *Report* (Albany: J. B. Lyon Company, 1930), 1:320. In the 1920s, the Second District Commission was succeeded by a single Public Service Commission which also assumed the regulatory duties of the First District Commission with the exception of New York City rapid transit problems.

4. Ibid.

5. Van Santvoord, *Chairman*, dissenting, *Re* Petition of Lockport Gas and Electric Company, VI P.S.C. 2nd D. 181, 186–84; colloquy, case 5681, pp. 8–9, roll 90, 2nd Dist. Minutes, Central Files, NYS PSC; colloquy, case 6595, p. 50, roll 109, ibid.

with its ability to build up a case law in the various fields under its jurisdiction.[6] The Commission's policies in the case law fields had seemed to New Yorkers to promote a state of fair dealing between consumer and corporation, and among the various interests of the business community. If a civic association, a consumer's league, a corporation, or an individual complainant had not been given all that it wanted from a Commission decision, it had at least been given acceptable reasons, grounded in law, why it was not entitled to more. But in the nonjusticiable fields, the Commission all along had been compelled to attempt to mediate disputes without the benefit of a rule for the case, and except in the field of railroad freight service, it had not been able to improve greatly upon the circumstances of 1907 by this means. Parties dissatisfied with a Commission initiative were quick to attribute it to Commission bias and to reject it out of hand. Thus, even at the beginning of 1913, New Yorkers' estimate of the Commission's performance was a mixed one, and they were quick to spot, and make much of, the decline after Stevens' departure.[7]

The cause of the Commission's troubles might have been obvious, but for the fact that Stevens had never publicized his judicial approach. Since 1907, New Yorkers had attributed the Commission's successes to the powers of its supposed "expertise," and they had been at a loss to understand why, therefore, this expertise did not make its mark in all the areas of the Commission's responsibility. Now, when the Commission's expertise seemed to have ceased operating entirely, New Yorkers became intent to discover what could be done to revive it.[8]

6. See p. 77, above.

7. William Anderson, *The Work of Public Service Commissions* (Minneapolis: University of Minnesota, 1913), 30; *New York Times*, January 12, 1913, pt. 2, p. 16; Delos F. Wilcox, "Effects of State Regulation upon the Municipal Ownership Movement," American Academy of Political and Social Science, *Annals*, 53 (1914): 71–84.

8. *New York Times*, May 8, 1914, p. 7; Delos F. Wilcox, "The Crisis in Public Service Regulation in New York," *National Municipal Review*, 4 (1915): 547–63; William E. Mosher, "Public Utilities and Their Recent Regu-

The problem, it was soon concluded, was that the Commission had become "Tammanyized": the appointees of governor Hughes had been replaced over time with men whose only recommendation for office appeared to be loyalty to party. While the commissioners of the Stevens era, whose expertise had shown itself only now and then, apparently had been experts of a middling sort, the present commissioners seemed incapable of being experts at all. Many New Yorkers now believed that they saw "the chief weaknesses of the commission movement. It was clear that if the commissions should come to be manned by men who were politicians in the usually accepted meaning of that term, their efficiency would be destroyed and they would merely get in the way of constructive progress."[9] Unless a restoration could be effected, many observers now despaired of the cause of public service regulation in New York State.[10]

That the Commission had never been animated by expertise, but by another approach entirely, was going unnoticed, of course. And in this regard, it is revealing to see what offices some of the Tammany appointees had occupied before coming to the Commission. They had been judges in the New York court system, and although they had not distinguished themselves on the bench, they had not occasioned any great scandal either. They had labored to the limit of their abilities, which for them was the minimum standard of competence that a critical profession demanded of its judges. Although capable of sustaining a judicial approach, it had been their good fortune upon leaving the bench to be presented with positions where they were not held by lawyers and reviewing courts to the standards of judicial office. In the words of one, "you un-

---

lation," in Alexander C. Flick, ed., *The History of New York State* (New York: Columbia University Press, 1935), 8:242–43.

9. Wilcox, "Crisis in Public Service Regulation," 547.

10. Delos F. Wilcox, "Experts, Ethics and Public Policy in Public Utilities," *National Municipal Review*, 6 (1917): 472–85; Styles P. Jones, "State Versus Local Regulation," American Academy of Political and Social Science, *Annals*, 53 (1914): 94; John Bauer, "Deadlock in Public Utility Regulation," *National Municipal Review*, 11 (1922): 24–25.

derstand the obligations of attorneys appearing before Commissioners, bodies that are not judicial, are not treated with the same serious thought of attendance that they would be in a court; and then of course Commissioners themselves are perhaps a little bit less rigid in their enforcement of rules as to attendance and as to hearings as compared with a court."[11] To commissioners of the Tammany type, expertise meant that they could take it easy.[12]

In time, this fact was hit upon by one group of the Commission's critics. Between 1915 and 1917, a joint committee of the New York legislature, known as the Thompson Committee, subjected the Second District Commission to a thorough investigation. Like other observers of the regulatory crisis in the Second District, the Committee found a situation where "final orders are hesitatingly entered, calmly disobeyed and quickly forgotten. Hearings are adjourned on the slightest pretext; the sitting commissioner, under a well-established plan of procedure, is constantly seeking adjustments or compromises of the immediately existing difficulty so that a final decision may be avoided."[13] What distinguished the Thompson Committee from other critics, however, was that it thought the cause of this behavior lay not in the personal characteristics of the commissioners themselves but in the fact that "the Commission has not created precedents." The Committee believed that it "too often happens that expression of discontent [with regulation] emphasizes too much the importance of the personal elements involved." But "the fault is not so much with the men as with the system employed."[14]

If one wished to understand the failings of the Second District Commission, one had to realize "first the weakness and inefficiency of the *legal system* under which the State of New

11. Testimony of Edward E. McCall, Joint Legislative Committee, *Final Report*, 1:299; McCall was a chairman of the First District Commission.

12. Testimony of Frank H. Mott, ibid., 2:1710; testimony of Devoe P. Hodson, ibid., 2:1982.

13. Joint Legislative Committee to Investigate the Public Service Commissions, *Complete Report* (Albany: J. B. Lyon Company, 1917), 118.

14. Ibid., 119, 156–57.

York for nearly ten years has been operating its experiment in supervising and controlling the services which are rendered to the public by various companies."[15] Consequently, the Thompson Committee proposed a reorganization of the Commission that would bring into focus its judicial function. The Commission was to be divided into a regulatory division, consisting of regulatory commissioners and administrative staff, and a hearing division, whose hearing commissioners would devote themselves entirely to adjudications. With one exception, the regulatory commissioners were to have all the authority of the old commissioners, including the power to hold hearings and issue final orders. This exception was where a justiciable controversy presented itself and either a party demanded an adjudication or the regulatory commissioner thought an adjudication advisable. Then the matter would be bound over to the hearing division. Decisions of the hearing division were to be reviewable on questions of both law and fact on appeal to the department of New York's intermediate appellate court that sat at Albany.[16]

By isolating and emphasizing the Commission's judicial function, the Thompson Committee was seeking to animate the administrative process in New York by means of the creation of an administrative jurisprudence. Its plan would formalize and make public the functional division of the Commission's work that had been accomplished informally and out of the public view in the Stevens era. Moreover, the plan would provide for a test of the reality and efficacy of a uniquely administrative expertise by separating the Commission into a judicial sphere and an "administrative" one. The Committee expected that the regulatory commissioners under the reorganization would carry out their responsibilities with a nonjudicial technique. Indeed, the Committee members were willing to believe that this technique might be truly "administrative"—that is, something that arose only from the circumstances of administrative government and its opportunity for

15. Ibid., 120.
16. Ibid., 139–65.

specialized knowledge. But if the purely "administrative" hearings held by the regulatory commissioners proved slow and inconclusive, if the commissioners were unable by some special technique to quell the constant shifting of opinions which had confounded Stevens at hearings of this type, and if the justiciable hearings held by the hearing commissioners seemed speedy and resolute in comparison, then new insights into the nature of administrative government might be gained.[17]

2

By the time that the Thompson Committee was finishing up its work in 1917, it was only one of many critics of the Commission. Indeed, over the next half-dozen years a variety of reorganization plans would be debated in New York. But now, at least, a judicial approach had been publicly formulated, and apparently so had an explicit challenge to Bruce Wyman's view of administrative government.

By the late teens, however, events in New York State were the least of Wyman's troubles. For a time after the appearance of his treatise in 1903, his life and work had gone smoothly enough. Indeed, in the decade following the publication of his treatise, Wyman became the most prominent legal scholar working in the field of administrative law and government. "I have written the two books most used by practitioners," he informed Roscoe Pound in 1913.[18] Moreover, "I would not be too modest to say that I have an established reputation in that field as an expert consulter."[19] Wyman practiced before the

17. Ibid., 120–47. One might add that a greater and more forthright reliance upon the judicial function in administration in the early decades of this century should have yielded a far greater understanding of the judge as policy-maker than we now possess. See Introduction, secs. 1, 2, and chap. 2, sec. 3, above, and Postscript, below.

18. Wyman to Pound, November 28, 1913, Pound MSS, box 231, folder 15, Harvard Law School Library.

19. "Mr. BRUCE WYMAN, Sworn," transcript of testimony before Massachusetts Public Service Commission (1913), p. 1, Pound MSS, box 231, folder 15.

Interstate Commerce Commission on behalf of numerous clients, was a prime mover in the creation of the Massachusetts Public Service Commission, and was the counsel for the National Civic Federation's influential study of public service regulation.[20] But it is clear from his writings that Wyman by about 1913 was becoming increasingly troubled by the adjudicative power of administrative bodies. The more he attempted to deal with this phenomenon, the more he came to describe it in terms that had disturbing implications for the traditional courts.[21]

By 1913, administrative adjudication disposed of so many legal controversies that Wyman could no longer describe its substantive determinations as only an "internal law" of the administration which "is from first to last an unfixed obligation, one way in one case, another in another, as expediency dictates."[22] Even in 1903, Wyman had hedged a bit on this proposition.[23] By 1913, he felt compelled to have the courts oversee administrative adjudication on a regular enough basis that practices "inconsistent with our notions of justice" would be quickly found out and eliminated.[24]

This did not seem to be much of an extension of the device of proceduralism that was a part of Wyman's scheme in 1903. But, given that administrative agencies had come to do the work of courts in the newer fields of litigation, Wyman was finding it difficult to confine practices "inconsistent with our notions of justice" to matters of administrative procedure.

20. Ibid., pp. 1–37; see also memorandum with letter from Wyman to Joseph H. Beale, January 2, 1914, Pound MSS, box 231, folder 15; *The Gas Age*, 31 (Feb. 15, 1913): 186–87.

21. Bruce Wyman, *Control of the Market* (New York: Moffat, Yard, 1911), 274–77; Bruce Wyman, "State Control of Public Utilities," *Harvard Law Review*, 24 (1911): 230–31; Bruce Wyman, "Unfair Competition by Monopolistic Corporations," American Academy of Political and Social Science, *Annals*, 42 (1912): 67–73.

22. Bruce Wyman, *Principles of Administrative Law* (St. Paul, Minn.: Keefe-Davidson, 1903), 13.

23. See pp. 70–71, above.

24. Bruce Wyman, "Jurisdictional Limitations upon Commission Action," *Harvard Law Review*, 27 (1914): 568.

Thus, by 1913, Wyman was maintaining that "as a people we will not be content to have our rights determined by administrative fiat; we demand reasoned judgment based upon ascertained principles generally understood. . . . We must have some objective standard to go upon, or we have no security from subjective differences."[25] This sounded fine, but the problem was that such a requirement tended to make the administration's discretion to decide controversies no freer or more variable than the permissible discretion of the courts; and it was precisely the variability of administrative determinations—of the "internal law"—that had allowed Wyman to claim in 1903 that the substance of administrative decisions was unfit for judicial review.[26]

Of course, the standards and principles applied in administrative adjudication did not necessarily have to be forged there, and in this event, substantive review became a less vital, or at least a less creative, task. The relevant standards and principles could have derived from statute, if legislatures had been able or disposed to define administrative programs in statutory detail. They could have derived from agency rulemaking,[27] if administrators had been able or disposed to define their purposes by that means. They could have derived from the intuitive flashes of expertise, if expertise had been able to reveal itself in the written word.

If administrative adjudication had been a process of the application of preexisting norms to the facts of a given case, an intensive review of administrative decisions in the continental fashion might well have acted more as a drag on administrative efficiency than as a clarifier of administrative purposes. But it was becoming clear by 1913 that administrators were proceeding to define their purposes, such as they were, almost wholly by means of adjudication. The practical choice for Wyman as a scholar analyzing a problem in government was whether a primitive judicialism should be acknowledged as

25. Ibid., 569.
26. See pp. 61–62, above.
27. That is, the making of agency regulations.

such and its implications for the courts investigated, or whether it should be treated as "administration," as something like the administration of the mid-nineteenth century in terms of the attention which courts, scholars, and law schools would devote to it. Wyman chose administration.[28]

For Wyman as a case-method scholar and as a common-law loyalist, this was a necessary choice. But it was not a particularly satisfactory one by the standards of modern analytical scholarship that the Harvard Law School faculty professed to follow. Wyman had set forth in great detail the elements of a scheme that sought to keep administrative agencies at arm's length from courts. But his approach was convincing only if it could be shown that administrative adjudication was different from that of the courts, and this Wyman failed to do in significant respects. Moreover, as a Langdellian, there seemed to be no avoiding this failure. Wyman's scholarly values were those of late nineteenth-century Harvard Law School scholarship, of Langdell and Ames. Unlike many later scholars, Wyman believed that rational principles of paramount importance were buried in the mass of case decisions in any given field of law. He had been saying that in administrative law the cases were beginning to yield their science, that there was "a consistent body of law in the process of unification."[29] By the standards of both the modern university and case-method scholarship, he had committed himself to stating a coherent and unified picture of his subject.[30]

Wyman was not yet forty in 1913, and it would have been interesting to see where the tensions of his scholarship might have taken him in the next decades. But at the end of 1913, he was forced to resign from the Harvard Law School, and

28. Wyman, "Jurisdictional Limitations," 569.

29. Bruce Wyman and Joseph Henry Beale, *Railroad Rate Regulation*, 2nd ed. by Bruce Wyman (New York: Baker, Voorhis, 1915), 30 (quotation); this work was in progress in 1913; also see pp. 31–33, 902–12.

30. Bruce Wyman, *Cases on Public Service Companies*, 2nd ed. (Cambridge: The Harvard Law Review Association, 1909), iv; Wyman, *Control of the Market*, 1–3, 274–77; Wyman, "State Control of Public Utilities," 625, 629.

except for finishing a few projects that were in progress at the time of his resignation, he wrote nothing more of consequence on administration. By the end of 1913, in fact, Wyman was something of a ruined man.

It had appeared in the press that Wyman had been making public speeches advocating the consolidation of the New England rail system and its regulation by a regional commission; and that he had been doing so in his capacity as a law professor and a legal expert without revealing to his audiences that he was under retainer to the New Haven Railroad. Since he had been making similar speeches before he went on the New Haven's retainer, Wyman felt that he had not acted unethically. But the press created a minor furor, particularly in light of the fact that the New Haven's president, Charles S. Mellen, had been attempting a takeover of the other New England railroads. In order not to embarrass the Law School, Wyman resigned. From 1914 onwards, he devoted himself to his consulting practice, while his friend and former colleague, Roscoe Pound, tried without success to locate a teaching position for him. Finally, Wyman took a part-time position at the Portia Law School, a walk-up institution for women in Boston. His fame and influence declined, and in the mid-twenties, still a relatively young man, he died.[31]

3

More important, perhaps, as Wyman's fortunes declined after 1913, those of Ernst Freund at last began to rise. For many years after Beale imposed the regime of pure law at Chicago, Freund had persevered in his opinions of what law was, how it should be taught, and what beyond the study of cases were the proper areas for the legal scholar's investiga-

31. Material on the Wyman affair may be found in the following collections: Pound MSS, box 231, folder 15, Harvard Law School Library; Ezra Ripley Thayer MSS, Harvard University Archives; Charles S. Mellen MSS, New Hampshire Historical Society (see Wyman to Mellen, October 17, 1913).

tion. After years of delay, he finally began to produce a scholarship reflecting his attitudes.

This work had to be conceived and written entirely in Freund's private hours, for when Beale returned to Harvard in 1904, the next dean proved to be only a little more liberal in his sense of what and how Freund might teach. Numerous courses that might have reinforced his scholarship and accelerated its appearance were excluded from the Law School's curriculum. Freund attempted to give them to undergraduates—a statutes course in 1907, courses on "principles of social and economic legislation" and "problems of state government" a few years later—but their content was too legalistic for non–law students, and he was forced to abandon them.[32] Since all of Freund's later writings were anticipated in their concerns and to some degree in their conclusions by short articles which he produced as early as 1894, it seems reasonable to conclude that he was slowed down considerably by the state of affairs at the Law School. As it was, it was not until the era of the First World War that his work achieved real forcefulness in its breadth of vision and complexity of argument.[33]

Freund's earliest premises, and ones which would remain

32. Freund was permitted by his law school colleagues to give his statutes course only after he had in essence compelled them to do so, by producing a major piece of scholarship on the subject. This was *Standards of American Legislation*, delivered as a series of lectures at Johns Hopkins in 1915 and brought out in book form in 1917. For Freund's problems with courses, see Freund to Helen Tunnicliff Catterall, October 29, 1917, Presidents' Papers 1889–1925, box 19, folder 6, University of Chicago Library (". . . the work which you did here in the early days was almost entirely non-professional, with the possible exception of constitutional and International Law. None of the courses which I then gave would now be offered as courses leading to the J. D. degree"); and in this regard, chap. 1, n. 84, above; see also, University of Chicago, *Annual Register*, 1902–3 through 1914–15 (Law School and Department of Political Science), and *Announcement, the Law School*, 1915–16 through 1918–19.

33. During this period, Freund was active as a consultant and advocate in matters of current legislation and social welfare, as well as administrative law; see Arthur H. Kent, "The Work of Ernst Freund in the Field of Legislation," *University of Chicago Law Review*, 1 (1933): 94–96; Jane Addams,

basic in his work to the end, were that legislation and administration were major elements of a legal order of a modern society and that therefore legal science must increasingly take note of them. In legal history, Freund stands for the proposition, very simply, that lawyers should think about government power. In his first work on administration, published in 1894, he observed that "the progress of civilization creates new spheres of administrative action in which the exercise of discretionary powers is indispensable,"[34] and in his last, published in 1932, he repeated a lifelong belief that "it is legitimate in an analytical study of administrative powers to differentiate grades of discretion and to attempt to discover their implications as regards desirability or undesirability of delegation, effect upon administrative practice, and amenability to judicial control."[35]

Without this effort, Freund believed, the course of the governmental expansion of the twentieth century lay, more or less, in the lap of the gods. He saw that many of his contemporaries understood that "the striking recourse to administrative powers . . . is due to . . . the inability of the legislature to formulate standards sufficiently definite for private guidance."[36] But he saw, too, their automatic assumption that, by getting into closer and more continuous contact with social and economic problems than a legislature could, the administrative agency would in time acquire an expertise that would enable it to formulate these standards.[37]

Was this a correct assumption? All Freund really asked of his fellow lawyers and legal scholars was that they think about

---

"The Friend and Guide of Social Workers," *University* [of Chicago] *Record*, 19 (1933): 43–45.

34. Ernst Freund, "The Law of the Administration in America," *Political Science Quarterly*, 9 (1894): 419.

35. Ernst Freund, *Legislative Regulation* (New York: Commonwealth Fund, 1932), 74.

36. Ernst Freund, *Administrative Powers over Persons and Property* (Chicago: University of Chicago Press, 1928), 29.

37. Ibid., 583.

it. Were the never-ending agency hearings really what they appeared to be, a "'trial-and-error' method of discovering a rule" for social and economic regulation? Or was this administrative process too often simply "a legislative makeshift to appease the demand for public control"?[38] If "administrative power is used for the purpose of experimenting with problems not as yet solved and perhaps for the present unsoluble, we must be prepared to take the consequences."[39]

It was clear to Freund, however, that no one as yet was prepared to do this, certainly not legal scholars. While they agreed that the administrative process lay within the modern legal order, they seemed to feel that their responsibility could be limited to the study of the regular court cases that reviewed administrative action on procedural grounds.[40] But it seemed to Freund that "if the legislature asks the administration to evolve standards in matters which cannot . . . be scientifically or legally standardized . . . no skill in devising procedural safeguards will produce just or beneficial results."[41] Among the various departments of the university that studied the administrative process, Freund believed that it was preeminently the responsibility of a law faculty to analyze the problems involved when a legislature told an administrative agency to govern in the "public interest." The understanding of the "complex mechanism of legal rights and remedies" required for this analysis "practically debars others than lawyers from effective constructive work in this direction, and unless legal science assumes the development of this aspect of the law, it cannot be expected to be accomplished with any degree of success."[42]

38. Ibid., 29.

39. Ernst Freund, "Historical Survey," in Ernst Freund et al., *The Growth of American Administrative Law* (St. Louis: Thomas Law Book Co., 1923), 39.

40. This point will be developed at length at chap. 4, sec. 2, below.

41. Freund, "Historical Survey," 38–39.

42. Ernst Freund, "The Correlation of Work for Higher Degrees in Graduate Schools and Law Schools," *Illinois Law Review*, 11 (1916): 308.

Yet, perhaps, Freund was being too pessimistic. For in this period, a number of dissents against the "pure law" values of the Harvard Law School were beginning to appear. Thus, William Draper Lewis, the dean of the University of Pennsylvania Law School, expressed his concern that "the graduates of our best university law schools seem . . . utterly lacking in any conception that the profession has any duties toward the community as a whole, or that they as individuals need concern themselves with any problems not met with in private practice";[43] and he found the reason for this in the Harvard model of legal education. "Look at the catalogue of any one of our great schools and you will see at a glance that the faculty have one and only one conception of their duty toward their students, and this is to turn them out able to answer any legal question likely to be put to them by private clients."[44] But in an era of expanding government regulation, the work of a lawyer, even on behalf of a private citizen, could involve questions of public policy and might involve appearances before tribunals that were not courts. How unfortunate, Lewis thought, that "ideals concerning legal education are in great part conscious or unconscious reflections of our conception of the functions of the lawyer and judge,—the nature of the work which they are called upon to do."[45] These had come from an earlier age, from the age of Langdell's youth, and were no longer sufficient to describe the various activities of the modern legal order.[46]

An even more sweeping indictment of Harvard's limitations

43. William Draper Lewis, "Legal Education and the Failure of the Bar to Perform its Public Duties," American Bar Association, *Reports*, 30 (1906): 2:46.

44. Ibid., 47.

45. William Draper Lewis, "The Social Sciences as the Basis of Legal Education," *University of Pennsylvania Law Review*, 61 (1913): 532.

46. For similar criticism, see Melville M. Bigelow, *Centralization and the Law* (Boston: Little, Brown, 1906), 14–19; William Carey Jones, "The Problem of the Law School," *California Law Review*, 1 (1912): 3. For a general analysis, see G. Edward White, *Tort Law in America* (New York: Oxford University Press, 1980), 64–75.

appeared in 1914 with the publication of the Redlich Report.[47] Written by Dr. Josef Redlich of the University of Vienna, it had been commissioned by the Carnegie Foundation for the Advancement of Teaching. The officers of the Foundation had supposed that "it would be difficult to obtain from any teacher of law or any practitioner of law in America a thoroughly sound, fair-minded, and scholarly report upon this question. We therefore turned to England and the Continent to see if some one could be found who would take up this enquiry in a sympathetic spirit, and who could bring to it the requisite educational and legal discrimination."[48]

Redlich in fact proved to be a very sympathetic observer. He was so impressed by the case method that in the final draft of his report some "of the effusiveness in regard to Harvard" had to be toned down by his editors.[49] But the case method impressed Redlich in terms of what he felt it was suited to—the analysis of cases—and his report tried to demonstrate that by itself this regimen did not meet the needs of legal education and the legal order.

Thus, Redlich confronted the law teachers of 1914 with something that Ames and Keener had always known: the case method and the catholic arguments in its behalf were often discrete. Redlich showed that, even though law teachers were still analogizing the case class to the scientific laboratory, the case method had been transformed in the 1880s from a means of supposedly achieving the scientific comprehension of the legal order to an end in itself; that instead of providing a scientific comprehension of law, it represented a rampant empiricism.[50] "The result of this is that the students never obtain a

47. Josef Redlich, *The Common Law and the Case Method* (New York: Carnegie Foundation for the Advancement of Teaching, 1914).

48. Henry S. Prichett, "Preface," in Redlich, *Case Method*, vi.

49. Alfred Z. Reed to Edward Brinley Adams, November 14, 1914, E. R. Thayer MSS, box 8, folder 8, Harvard Law School Library; Reed was the director of the Carnegie Foundation's inquiry into legal education and Adams was the Harvard Law School librarian.

50. Redlich, *Case Method*, 23–28, 41–57.

general picture of the law as a whole, not even a picture which includes only its main features. This is . . . however . . . a task which should be accomplished by the law courses in the universities."[51] Only if law teachers undertook "to try to reveal to the younger generation in the law schools the true problems of the common law and of modern legal development in general"[52] would American law "prove equal to its next great task, inexorably imposed upon it by the modern organization of a completely industrialized democracy."[53]

This was not what law teachers after the Harvard fashion wanted to hear. Thus, Ezra Ripley Thayer, Ames' successor as dean at Harvard, wrote to friends, "I think none of us are enthusiastic about the idea of an investigation by a foreigner."[54] But "I gather that the Carnegie people are bent upon having this done, and I do not see anything for the rest of us to do but submit and look pleasant."[55] So following his own advice, Thayer informed the Carnegie Foundation of his "desire to get the immediate benefit of Professor Redlich's suggestions in my own personal instruction,"[56] although privately he deplored "the general principle of calling in Germans to pass on American instruction."[57]

Indeed, among the Harvard faculty, the rising tide of criticism was felt most acutely by Thayer, and in fact it would contribute to his suicide in 1915. For emotionally, Thayer was a Langdellian. He was the son of the illustrious James Bradley

51. Ibid., 41.

52. Ibid., 65.

53. Ibid., 66.

54. Thayer to Henry M. Bates, October 17, 1913, E. R. Thayer MSS, box 9, folder 2.

55. Thayer to Charles Noble Gregory, October 8, 1913, ibid.

56. Thayer to Alfred Z. Reed, October 20, 1914, E. R. Thayer MSS, box 8, folder 8.

57. Thayer to Harlan F. Stone, October 8, 1913, E. R. Thayer MSS, box 9, folder 2; for similar reactions, see Harlan F. Stone, "Dr. Redlich on the Case Method in American University Law Schools," *Columbia University Quarterly*, 17 (1915): 262–73; Joseph H. Beale, "The Law School as Professor Redlich Saw It," *Harvard Graduates' Magazine*, 23 (1915): 617–20; the Redlich Report will be discussed further in chap. 4, sec. 2, below.

Thayer and had been raised in the atmosphere of the Harvard Law School during Langdell's deanship. He had expected to become a lawyer and had done so. Twice he had elected to remain in practice rather than accept offers from the Law School to join the faculty. He had hoped for an eventual appointment to the bench, and he had only returned to the Law School out of a sense of duty when Ames died and the deanship fell open. Intellectually, however, Thayer was a man who could not avoid seeing the changes that were taking place in the law and that dated the attitudes of the early 1890s. Even in the year of his graduation, 1891, he had written about the judicial function in a way that revealed its similarity to the adjudicative power of administrators, although at the time he was not conscious of having done this. But by 1910, when he became dean, it would have been difficult for Thayer not to see the similarity.[58]

By 1910, confronting the changes that were overtaking the law had become as much a task for a dean as it was for a scholar like Wyman who worked in the newer fields of law; for the nature of modern law, or at least the world's perception of it, would ultimately determine what the Harvard Law School, as a law school, must be about. Thus, it seemed to Thayer that as dean he was constantly engaged in "preserving the spirit of the common law against threatening dangers."[59] For instance, there was the issue of whether jurisprudence was a fit subject to be taught in a law school. On the surface, this appeared to be a minor matter, but it was one with a threatening potential. Jurisprudence pushed student and teacher alike in the direction of seeing the law as a whole, of seeing the relative importance of its subdivisions, and the preoccupations of the Harvard Law School did not fare well from this vantage. Jurisprudence was one of the thrusts, and one of the dangers, of

58. Arthur E. Sutherland, *The Law at Harvard* (Cambridge: The Belknap Press of Harvard University Press, 1967), 231–32; Ezra R. Thayer, "Judicial Legislation: Its Legitimate Function in the Development of the Common Law," *Harvard Law Review*, 5 (1891): 172–201.

59. Ezra Ripley Thayer, "Looking Ahead," *Harvard Alumni Bulletin*, 17 (1914): 104.

the Redlich Report, and Redlich was not alone in calling for a more intellectual study of law. Thayer's correspondence was filled with thrusts and parries on this question. Even the editors of the *Harvard Law Review* petitioned him for the creation of a "Theory of Law" course, so that as practitioners they might "assist intelligently in causing those changes in our law which are desirable."[60]

Thayer wished to be loyal to the spirit of the common law and to the case method, but he could not simply brush aside the implications of a changing legal order. As dean, he tried to effect compromises between these two impulses and to accommodate both the law's past and its future. Thus, he implemented a plan for an optional fourth year of study which was to contain everything that was new or opposed to the spirit of the basic three-year curriculum: jurisprudence and administrative law and non–case-method offerings. In this way, he hoped, the Harvard Law School as an institution might pay homage to change, while leaving its individual members free to ignore it. But by 1915, only four students were enrolled for a fourth year, and the program had done little to relieve the pressures for change on the three-year curriculum and on Thayer as its guardian against "threatening dangers."[61]

By the end of the decade, it was evident that the example of Harvard's fourth year had not prevented other law schools from apparently adopting both the letter and the spirit of Redlich's suggestions. According to Arthur Corbin of Yale, there were arising "new types of legal scholars and investigators" who were aware "that there are other sources than the court

60. Petition from editors of *Harvard Law Review* to Thayer, n.d., Thayer MSS, "Courses 1911–1914," Harvard University Archives. (By permission of the Harvard University Archives.) There are numerous items of a similar nature in the Thayer collections at the Archives and the Harvard Law School; see William Chase, "American Legal Scholarship and Administrative Law" (Ph.D. diss., Harvard University, 1978), at p. 266. For the dangers of jurisprudence, see Albert Kocourek, "Jurisprudence as an Undergraduate Study," *California Law Review*, 8 (1920): 232.

61. Samuel Williston, *Life and Law* (Boston: Little, Brown, 1940), 187–88; Sutherland, *Law at Harvard*, 232–34.

decisions."[62] They were beginning to lead their schools toward curricula and a sense of law that would have dismayed Ames every bit as much as Freund's ideas had in 1902. "Realism," "law and the social sciences," and "administrative law" were beginning to enter the vocabulary of legal education. In a few more years, schools like Yale and Columbia would fancy that they had passed Harvard by, and even some among the Harvard faculty would agree. It had seemed to Edward H. Warren that "the School was *facile princeps* among American law schools" when he joined the faculty in 1904, but it was becoming apparent to him that this was no longer so.[63]

And it was in this new atmosphere, after nearly two decades of Harvard orthodoxy, that Freund was finally presented with a major opportunity. In 1918, the Commonwealth Fund was established to promote "the welfare of mankind,"[64] and in 1920 its directors decided to support, among other things, projects in legal research. In 1921, a Committee on Administrative Law and Practice was created to direct one of these projects, with Freund as its chairman, and, eventually, Felix Frankfurter of the Harvard Law School, Frank J. Goodnow, by then president of Johns Hopkins, and Walter L. Fisher, a Chicago practitioner, as its other members. The task of the committee was thought to be nothing less than to foster the scholarship which would define authoritatively the fundamental legal issues of American administration. Its research was to be issued under auspices that would compel the attention of the legal profession. Freund's committee was to work under a parent Legal Research Committee that was composed of such luminaries as Benjamin Cardozo, Roscoe Pound, Harlan F.

62. Arthur L. Corbin, "Yale and the New Science of Jurisprudence," *Case and Comment*, 21 (1915): 953, 954.

63. Edward H. Warren, *Spartan Education* (Boston: Houghton Mifflin, 1942), 55; also see, White, *Tort Law*, 64–75.

64. *The New Columbia Encyclopedia* (New York: Columbia University Press, 1975), 611.

Stone, and, later in the decade, Charles Evans Hughes, along with a number of eminent practitioners.[65]

Thus, for the first time since the founding of the University of Chicago Law School, Freund had a chance to exert an influence of institutional proportions on the development of administrative government. "The inquiry has been my main thought during the last months," he wrote at the end of 1921.[66] The committee met for the first time on December 30, 1921, in Chicago, and Freund presented its members with a thirty-five-page "Working Plan" outlining what he felt should be their priorities. He assumed that he, as chairman, would be able to set priorities, and indeed he had already had some success along this line. In creating the administrative law committee, the parent Legal Research Committee had voted to confine the inquiry to "the topic of Administrative Procedures affecting Private Rights." But by the time of the December conference, Freund had been able to push the concept of the committee away from the strictly procedural by having it renamed an "Inquiry into Administrative Law and Practice."[67]

At the conference, Freund informed the committee members of his desire to investigate the "legitimate sphere and extent of administrative discretion,"[68] and to accomplish this by means of both field studies of individual agencies and a general survey of the administrative process. Above all,

65. Freund, *Administrative Powers*, v–vi; James Parker Hall to Felix Frankfurter, August 31, 1921, and Freund to Hall, January 9, 1922, Frankfurter Library of Congress microfilm, Harvard Law School Library; draft letters from Freund to Max Farrand, n.d., Freund MSS, box 2 addenda, "Commonwealth Fund," University of Chicago Library; Hall was chairman of the parent committee and dean of the Chicago Law School; Farrand was a sometime director of, sometime advisor to the Commonwealth Fund.

66. Draft of letter from Freund to Frankfurter ("Farrand suggests . . ."), n.d., Freund MSS, box 2 addenda, "Commonwealth Fund."

67. Freund, "Suggestion of a Working Plan for the Proposed Inquiry into Administrative Law and Practice under the Auspices of the Commonwealth Fund," Frankfurter Library of Congress microfilm; the original objectives were stated by Hall in his letter to Frankfurter of August 31, ibid.

68. Freund, "Suggestion of a Working Plan," p. 5, Frankfurter Library of Congress microfilm.

Freund thought it important to give the legal profession an overall picture of contemporary administrative law and practice by means of the general survey, and therefore he intended to keep this project for himself. Frankfurter had already made it clear that he was interested in directing the field studies. Some members wanted a greater emphasis on the study of judicial decisions, but Freund came away from the conference with the impression that the members had generally supported his outline for the inquiry. If he could continue to control the committee, the prospects seemed excellent for reversing the course of legal scholarship's contribution to the rising administrative process.[69]

69. Draft letters from Freund to Farrand, n.d., Freund MSS, box 2 addenda, "Commonwealth Fund" (there are two such letters that obviously date from this period); Freund memoranda, "The Three Days' Conference," and "Year End Conferences 1921/22," ibid.

4

"You Will Find Yourself in an Intellectual Fog Now": 1921–32

1

Even before the Chicago conference, Felix Frankfurter was moving toward cutting down the importance of Freund's general survey and the comprehensiveness of the entire inquiry.[1] Frankfurter, who was Bruce Wyman's replacement at the Harvard Law School, was soon to embark upon a decade-long rivalry with Freund for influence in the study and analysis of administrative government. According to Freund, only two days after the conference concluded Frankfurter became "increasingly insistent upon the paramount importance of the intensive studies, to which he apparently wishes to confine the inquiry for the present, and increasingly skeptical regarding the present value of anything like a comprehensive survey."[2] Later Frankfurter would insist that Freund's comprehensive approach represented "an undue quest for certainty" before conditions of legal development were ripe for a synthesis.[3]

As this opposition became clear, Freund did not dispute the need for Frankfurter's field studies. But "I am not as confident

1. Max Farrand to Felix Frankfurter, December 14, 1921, Frankfurter Library of Congress microfilm, Harvard Law School Library. ("Thank you very much for your very clear letter regarding Freund's outline. We are in absolute accord and I hope you have written strongly to Freund.")

2. Freund memorandum, "Comment on Frankfurter's Letter of January 4," Freund MSS, box 2 addenda, "Commonwealth Fund," University of Chicago Library; also see draft letter, Freund to Farrand ("Memorandum regarding meeting at New Haven, May 11, 1922"), ibid.

3. Felix Frankfurter, review of Ernst Freund et al., *The Growth of American Administrative Law* (1923), in *Harvard Law Review*, 37 (1924): 640.

as he is as to the result to be expected." The relatively unformed nature of the subject seemed to make a sense of its possibilities all the more important. The committee "must plan the inquiry so that the main problems of Administrative Law will at least be stated; no one expects that they will be finally solved." As for the field studies, "it may be that a mass of statistical and factual material will result in scientific demonstration of the merits or demerits of administrative practices . . . but it may also be that the material will be inadequate to support 'scientific' generalizations." Freund had assumed that "the committee regarded the proposed inquiry not primarily as an experiment in legal research, but was mainly interested in a problem of present day law and government."[4]

What Frankfurter was really after, Freund thought, was the preservation of the established routines of the university law school and legal scholarship.[5] Frankfurter's approach to the inquiry was well suited to this end, but if administrative law and government were the ends, then "the great need is a mapping out of the field and an agreement about the practical problems and the form in which they should be stated."[6]

4. Freund memorandum, "Comment on Frankfurter's Letter of January 4."

5. Freund, "Memorandum on Frankfurter's Letter" (pertaining to the letter of January 4, 1922, but a different memorandum from that cited in notes 2 and 4, above), Freund MSS, box 2 addenda, "Commonwealth Fund"; also see Freund, "The study of judicial decisions as a part of the Administrative Law and practice inquiry," ibid. Freund agreed to some extent with Frankfurter about the treatment of administrative law as an academic subject; see "Seminar Papers," ibid.

Another aspect of Frankfurter's opposition is suggested by H. N. Hirsch: that psychologically Frankfurter simply "could not accept serious, sustained opposition in fields he considered his domain of expertise," for he "had staked his psychological well-being on success and achievement—on 'winning.'" Frankfurter's neurosis was such that he could believe himself "a courageous, forthright, 'disinterested' scholar" at the same time that he indulged "his penchant for behind-the-scenes maneuvering." See H. N. Hirsch, *The Enigma of Felix Frankfurter* (New York: Basic Books, 1981), 5–6, 205, 97, 206 (quotations).

6. Freund memorandum, "Comment on Frankfurter's Letter of January 4."

Accordingly, Freund was determined to continue with the survey.

In opposition, Frankfurter was not entirely unyielding. As Freund's work began to appear, he conceded that Freund's readers "must surely have shifted a good deal of their mental scenery of the law" as a result of his comprehensive approach. "Naïf assumptions about Anglo-American law in its traditional application through courts are gently given their setting in the gradual extension of non-judicial (*i.e.*, non-court) legal control."[7] But Frankfurter insisted that no revision of institutional routines, in law or in law schools, need come of this. What Freund's work amounted to was only "far-flung generalized speculation regarding the administrative process and its relation to the traditional legal system."[8] His readers should realize that the problems he addressed "are still in the embryonic stage of development." Instead of following Freund's leads, Frankfurter suggested that it was both better and inevitable "that you will find yourself in an intellectual fog now. . . . I think we are in the fog of inadequate experience, we are as yet in a totally immature stage for suggesting wholesale remedies or large systems."[9] Legal scholarship should be content with the field studies that would come of the committee's work and not grope for a larger picture. Nothing need change. Only after many decades, or longer, would a comprehensive picture emerge from the accumulation of field studies, and then institutional routines could be revised. For Frankfurter, the value of the Commonwealth Fund inquiry was that, if his views prevailed, it would give the stamp of approval to this approach.[10]

7. Frankfurter review of *Growth of American Administrative Law*, 640.

8. Felix Frankfurter, introduction to "A Symposium on Administrative Law," *Iowa Law Review*, 18 (1933): 131.

9. Remarks of Frankfurter, "Report of the Cincinnati Conference on Functions and Procedure of Administrative Tribunals," *University of Cincinnati Law Review*, 12 (1938): 261, 271.

10. Frankfurter to Max Farrand, June 8, 1926, Frankfurter Library of Congress microfilm. ("With good reason you ought not to feel that the progress has been too slow. . . . I think that the output is serving two aims . . . namely, to make specific contributions to the development of administrative

In this effort, Frankfurter was aided by more than just his talent for breezy obfuscation. Rather, he had the support of the scholarly tradition that had been begun by Bruce Wyman at the turn of the century. By the time of his fall from grace, Wyman had been hard pressed to explain away the newer realities of administrative government, but in the years since 1914, Frankfurter had found a way to sustain Wyman's plausibility. This was to mate Wyman's work with that of Roscoe Pound.

This was ironic, in a sense. Pound was the one teacher of law at Harvard who seemed to belong in spirit to the modern university, and to be most removed from the spirit of the law school as merely a practitioner's college. Indeed, during the Progressive Era, among conservative members of the bar he had a reputation as a radical—as a man who wished to overturn established notions about the nature of law and the judicial function and to replace them with the fierce-sounding conception, "social engineering." It has been said of him that "in the process of re-examination and re-interpretation of the legacy of the common law, Pound takes on the stature of a colossus."[11] Nevertheless, Roscoe Pound was thoroughly a Harvard Law School man. He had once written darkly to Freund about "you administrative law people,"[12] and he never gave himself to any endeavor either at this time or in his later career that would have caused substantial modifications in Harvard's institutional routine. Indeed, to protect that routine

law and also through these specific contributions to set examples for work to be done by others.")

11. J. Forrester Davison and Nathan D. Grundstein, *Administrative Law and the Regulatory System*, rev. ed. (Washington: Lerner Law Book Co., 1968), 3.

12. Ernst Freund to Roscoe Pound, October 13, 1913, Pound MSS, box 221, folder 5, Harvard Law School Library. ("You speak of 'you administrative law people.' I can assure you that there are mighty few of us and a very different type from what you imagine. *Administrative Law* stands not for administrative power but for control of administrative power, and if we favor delegation it is only because we believe that control of delegated powers is more capable of development than control of legislation.")

and the conceptions of law and the judicial function that it depended upon, Pound willingly sacrificed consistency and comprehensiveness in his scholarship, and eventually, intellectual vitality—although not before providing Frankfurter with the insights he needed.[13]

Pound became interested in administrative agencies around 1905, and his conceptual problems with them plagued him thereafter in his career. Initially, he viewed administrative agencies as alien in every respect to courts, an attitude that he would return to during the New Deal. "Executive justice is an evil," he wrote in 1907. "It has always been and it always will be crude and as variable as the personalities of officials." In contrast, judicial justice centered on rule and principle, and "nothing but rule and principle, steadfastly adhered to, can stand between the citizen and official incompetency, caprice, or corruption." Thus, Pound concurred with Wyman's portrait of a variable administrative process and a fixed, rule-oriented judicial process, but not with Wyman's sense of the essential legitimacy of the administration's justice. For Pound at this time, there seemed to be little need for administrative agencies to adjudicate controversies if only the judges of the regular courts would cast off the sterile abstractions of a nineteenth-century jurisprudence and take into account the realities of the modern world. This "recrudescence of executive justice [is] one of those reversions to justice without law which are perennial in legal history and serve, whenever a legal system fails for the time being to fulfill its purpose, to infuse into it enough of current morality to preserve its life."[14]

But from 1907 to about 1920, Pound's view of administrative agencies as transient and ill-fitted usurpers of the judicial function shifted hesitatingly and never completely toward the view that these agencies were "apparently a permanent phenomenon" and that perhaps they could be justified as such.

13. David Wigdor, *Roscoe Pound: Philosopher of Law* (Westport, Conn.: Greenwood Press, 1974), 47, 156, 209, 221, 224, 231; Jerome Frank, *If Men Were Angels* (New York: Harper, 1942), 33ff.

14. Roscoe Pound, "Executive Justice," *The American Law Register*, 46 (1907): 144–46.

For upon closer examination, the nature of their adjudication did not seem to be so different from that of the courts—not, however, because Pound had discovered that administrators had come to rely on rule and principle, but because he had discovered that judges often did not. "Much of our difficulty in discussions of this subject comes from thinking of the modern law as made up wholly of rules. . . . But in truth a modern legal system is much more complex." "When putting aside the fictions of legal tradition, we look squarely at what actually takes place in the judicial and juristic development of legal materials, we need not fear for constitutional liberty because the commissions to which the application of so many legal standards is now committed do not proceed by the exact and certain methods of legal logic."[15]

Like other legal scholars in the early twentieth century, Pound had come to view administrative and judicial decision-making in the process of adjudication as remarkably alike. This similarity lessened Pound's concern about the danger to "constitutional liberty" posed by administrative agencies, but at the same time it was a more troubling insight, for Pound could not shake the feeling that somehow only the traditional courts were truly legitimate.[16]

Initially, Pound did not fully realize the source of his feeling. Before he had become interested in the problem of the administrative agency's place in the legal order, Pound had thought that all such problems were capable of being analyzed and resolved by legal scholars working out of the recently triumphant university law schools. "To my mind," he wrote in 1905, "the remedy is in our law schools."[17] But between 1905 and 1912, this attitude began to change. His analysis of the place of administrative agencies in the legal order, as of its other novel elements, conflicted with his feeling for the tra-

15. Roscoe Pound, "The Administrative Application of Legal Standards," American Bar Association, *Reports*, 44 (1919): 445, 454, 462.

16. Wigdor, *Pound*, 110, 139–41; Fred V. Cahill, Jr., *Judicial Legislation* (New York: Ronald Press, 1952), 81–82.

17. Roscoe Pound, "Do We Need a Philosophy of Law?" *Columbia Law Review*, 5 (1905): 352.

ditional courts and for the life of teaching and scholarship that was built upon court cases and institutionalized by the university law schools. Administrative agencies that did the work of courts and that might be permanent in the legal order presumably needed to be studied like courts, and this was an upsetting prospect. In practical effect, Pound was forced to choose between comprehensive scholarship and institutional loyalty, between analysis and the conflicting demands of a case-method tradition.[18]

Pound chose the latter, but in doing so he found that he did not have to sacrifice entirely the sensation that he was partaking of the former. Wyman, who had worked in very close focus with administrative government, had found that he could not satisfactorily distinguish administrative adjudication from the adjudication of the courts. This was distressing to anyone who was committed to the traditional judicial order, and who at the same time professed to be an analytical scholar. But Pound was able to lessen this tension simply by viewing the development of the administrative process from a distance. By placing it in the broad context of a legal order evolving experimentally over past, present, and future time, he was able to lessen, although not eliminate, the concern that the judicial power of administrative agencies caused legal scholars to feel.[19]

Pound was the first to see that it really did not matter, or at least it mattered less, that administrative agencies possessed the judicial power if ultimately their jurisprudence and their responsibilities could be absorbed by the regular courts, and if, in the meantime, the relationship between agencies and courts could be viewed pragmatically. The very fact that "executive justice" was recrudescent—that it had flared up and subsided in the past—suggested that its current manifestation

18. Roscoe Pound, "Taught Law," American Bar Association, *Reports*, 37 (1912): 975–96; Wigdor, *Pound*, 47, 139–41, 209, 221, 231.

19. With regard to this concern, see James O. Freedman, "Crisis and Legitimacy in the Administrative Process," *Stanford Law Review*, 27 (1975): 1041–45.

would ultimately subside.[20] In 1907, when Pound had viewed administrative adjudication as wholly an evil, he had wanted this to happen in the very near future. But now that he was disposed to view administrative adjudication in less dire terms, this future could be more distant.

Thus, legal scholars really did not need to exercise themselves over this phenomenon. It was not an evil that had to be confronted and eliminated without hesitation, and its similarity to the adjudication of the courts was not a call to action either because "executive justice" would not be permanent.[21] Moreover, Pound, like many members of the early twentieth-century university, was influenced by the philosophy of pragmatism, with its emphasis on the tentative and experimental nature of human understanding. From this perspective, the present implications of administrative adjudication could be said to be problematical at best. When administrative adjudication was looked at in this way, the legal scholar felt substantially better about it. He could ask open-ended questions about its place in the legal order, and be comforted by finding that matters were too indeterminate for drawing many conclusions. He could think himself loyal to the scholarly tenets of the modern university at the same time that he was being loyal to the judicentric traditions of the common law.[22]

Still, this was never quite enough for Pound. He remained uncomfortable about the power and standing that was given to the administrative process by Wyman's approach. Within a decade, he began to drift back to his original view of admin-

20. Pound, "Executive Justice," 144–45.

21. Roscoe Pound, "Justice According to Law," pt. 1, *Columbia Law Review*, 13 (1913): 696, 704–5, 713, and pts. 2–3, *Columbia Law Review*, 14 (1914): 4–7, 14–15, 18–25, 116–21.

22. Ibid., pt. 2, pp. 4–7, pt. 3, pp. 116–21; also see Edwin W. Patterson, *Jurisprudence: Men and Ideas of the Law* (Brooklyn: Foundation Press, 1953), 90, 465–74; Morton G. White, *Social Thought in America: The Revolt Against Formalism* (New York: Viking, 1949), 57, 240–41; Wigdor, *Pound*, 183ff.; G. Edward White, "From Sociological Jurisprudence to Realism: Jurisprudence and Social Change in Early Twentieth-Century America," *Virginia Law Review*, 58 (1972): 999–1028.

istrative agencies as usurpers of the judicial function. But by this time, Felix Frankfurter, who had arrived in the fall of 1914, was Harvard's leading influence in the field.[23]

Frankfurter contributed little more than a mood, but it was to be the essential prop of the whole apparatus as it had evolved by the 1920s. What Frankfurter did, very simply, was to use Pound to sustain Wyman.[24] This was the Pound of the Progressive Era, and in Frankfurter's hands Pound's idea about the ultimate absorption of the administrative process by courts became a marvelous alchemy. It transmuted the legal scholar who was committed to Wyman's scheme of avoidance into a habitué of the administrative process, into a university scholar eager for "an opportunity to modernize jurisprudence to serve the nation's industrial and economic needs."[25] Such a man made it a point to be informed of developments in the administrative process and the workings of its expertise. His senses told him that he was "in the presence of a movement as legitimate, as powerful, as pervasive as the movement which led to the establishment of courts of equity alongside courts of the common law."[26] In the same way that equity was

23. Frank, *If Men Were Angels*, 33ff.; Arthur E. Sutherland, *The Law at Harvard* (Cambridge: The Belknap Press of Harvard University Press, 1967), 240, 242.

24. The Pound and Wyman influences are evident in Felix Frankfurter, "The Law School and the Public Service," *Harvard Alumni Bulletin*, 17 (1914): 116; Frankfurter, "The Law and the Law Schools," American Bar Association, *Reports*, 41 (1915): 369–70; Frankfurter lecture notes for Public Utilities course, September 28, 1914, Frankfurter MSS, box 188, folder 2, Harvard Law School Library (here Frankfurter speaks of the "rules which the court and the legislature have to work out" [but not administrative agencies], as well as the Poundian concern "that the old lawyers and judges are [not] equipped for the task that is at hand").

25. Jerold S. Auerbach, "Enmity and Amity: Law Teachers and Practitioners, 1900–1922," *Perspectives in American History*, 5 (1971): 560 (quotation); also see Frankfurter, "Law School and Public Service," 115–16; Felix Frankfurter, "The Utilities Bureau," American Academy of Political and Social Science, *Annals*, 57 (1915); 293–94.

26. Remarks of Frankfurter, "Report of Cincinnati Conference," 365.

eventually absorbed by the common law, he could see the advent of administrative courts and the substantive review of administrative decisions.[27]

But he could see all this, and be made to feel intellectually in vogue for having seen it, and yet know that for the present nothing in the Wyman scheme would change. For "in administrative law we are dealing pre-eminently with law in the making; with fluid tendencies and tentative traditions. Here we must be especially wary against the danger of premature synthesis, of sterile generalization unnourished by the realities of 'law in action.'"[28] Instead of pursuing "an undue quest for certainty"[29] after the fashion of Ernst Freund, the true scholar must be content with knowing that field studies, such as those sponsored by the Commonwealth Fund, were monitoring these realities. "We must have many such before many generalizations about regulation can be hazarded."[30] The day of Poundian absorption was far in the future, and for the present, enthusiasm for expertise and Wyman's scheme would suffice.[31]

27. Frankfurter to William D. Guthrie, December 22, 1922, Frankfurter MSS, box 188, folder 2 (where Frankfurter agrees with Guthrie's view that ultimately there will be administrative courts in America); Felix Frankfurter and James M. Landis, *The Business of the Supreme Court* (New York: Macmillan, 1928), 184–86.

28. Felix Frankfurter, "The Task of Administrative Law" (1927), in Archibald MacLeish and E. F. Prichard, ed., *Law and Politics, Occasional Papers of Felix Frankfurter, 1913–1938* (New York: Harcourt, Brace, 1939), 236.

29. Frankfurter review of *Growth of American Administrative Law*, 640.

30. Felix Frankfurter, "Introduction," in Morris Llewellyn Cooke, ed., *Public Utility Regulation* (New York: Ronald Press, 1924), 3.

31. Felix Frankfurter, "The Conditions for, and the Aims and Methods of, Legal Research" (1930), in MacLeish and Prichard, *Law and Politics*, 287–98; Frankfurter, "Task of Administrative Law," ibid., 237; Frankfurter, "General Introduction," in Edwin Wilhite Patterson, *The Insurance Commissioner in the United States* (Cambridge: Harvard University Press, 1927); Frankfurter to William Draper Lewis, May 1, 1929, Thomas Reed Powell MSS, box A-1, Harvard Law School Library ("the domain of public law . . . is not remotely ripe for harvesting. . . . That means a total absence of pressure for quick results, a total lack of the urgencies of immediacy"). I think it

2

In his struggle against Freund, Frankfurter had concocted a rationale of dazzling surface beauty. But would it play in the brave new world of legal education in the twenties? The tide of threatening dangers that had so dismayed Ezra Ripley Thayer in 1915 continued to rise in the decade after his death, and the times seemed all opposed to the scholarship of avoidance that lay at the heart of Frankfurter's appeal.

Yet, though they could not see it, law teachers at schools like Columbia and Yale had deviated very little in matters of substance from the Harvard model, and this fact would be of inestimable value to Frankfurter in his struggle with Freund. Breaking with "Harvard" had meant replacing, a little sooner than Harvard did, an older conception of the nature of judge-made law with a newer one, or using a little earlier social science materials to supplement the study of cases. But the experience of the case class remained the balance wheel of the professional law teacher's existence, determining for him what was "strictly legal" and what he should be about in his scholarship. Thus, for the Columbia faculty in the 1920s, their course experiments were ones in law *and* the social sciences—the dimension of "law" remained little changed in practical effect. So also, the realists of the 1930s directed their skepticism to regular-court cases and few others. As for the additions of courses in administrative law, one professor noted:

> The numerous existing two hour one semester courses in administrative law are justified on a number of bases, but aside from a vague interest and desire on the part of the school heads to have course titles listed in the catalogue which prove that their curricula are keeping pace with the times, perhaps the most powerful factor in introducing this type of administrative law course has been to permit the new [teacher] to give one of his recent sets of notes to his class, verbally, and call it administrative law, in order that he may have the

---

is fair to say that the Frankfurter correspondence abounds with sentiments such as the ones found in the Lewis letter; see William Chase, "American Legal Scholarship and Administrative Law" (Ph.D. diss., Harvard University, 1978), at pp. 277–81.

remainder of his time to work up what are considered real law courses. . . . Two hours was not too much to indulge the young man, under the circumstances, and at any rate the course would be passed on to the next new staff member when he came along.[32]

Such departures from Harvard orthodoxy at best served to give to lesser schools a sense of institutional identity after a period of overwhelming Harvard dominance in legal education. But the basic orientation which Ames gave to law study in the 1880s by promoting the case method endured. Administrative law was still taught by means of cases of the reviewing courts, and law in general—whether it was thought of as objective rule or subjective value preference—was still primarily the case law of the regular courts. Indeed, a modern observer notes that from an almost total absorption in reading court cases, law teachers still "derive their notions of what is important. . . . A type-situation that gives rise to two or three appellate cases a year, particularly if the decisions seem muddled and inconsistent, becomes an 'important problem' to the reader, regardless of what it means to the outside world."[33]

32. Oliver P. Field, "The Study of Administrative Law: A Review and a Proposal," *Iowa Law Review*, 18 (1933): 239 (quotation); also see Robert B. Stevens, "Two Cheers for 1870: The American Law School," *Perspectives in American History*, 5 (1971): 470–542; G. Edward White, *Tort Law in America* (New York: Oxford University Press, 1980), 63, 71–73; Sutherland, *Law at Harvard*, 226–312; Samuel Williston, *Life and Law* (Boston: Little, Brown, 1940), 187–91.

33. Lawrence M. Friedman, "Law Reform in Historical Perspective," *St. Louis University Law Journal*, 13 (1969), 356 (quotation).

The judicial tunnel-vision of the "new" model law teachers at Columbia and Yale is exemplified by a complaint against the limitations of the "law and social science" exercise made by Robert Hutchins, the dean of the Yale Law School in the late 1920s: "The fact was that though the social scientists seemed to have a great deal of information, we could not see and they could not tell us how to use it. It did not seem to show us what the courts would do or whether what they would do was right." Quoted in John W. Johnson, *American Legal Culture, 1908–1940* (Westport, Conn.: Greenwood Press, 1981), at p. 99. Johnson discusses the research of the new model law professors of the late 1920s and early 1930s, and with the exception of some of the work of Underhill Moore, all of it was concerned exclusively with the regular judicial process. See ibid., 101–6.

Only rarely had Harvard's critics proposed abolishing the case method itself. As law teachers at other schools strove to differentiate their programs from the Harvard model, their allegiance to its one essential, the case method, grew stronger in fact. Indeed, by 1920, there might be said to have been a second victory of the case method in the world of legal education. The first, the victory of 1903, had been achieved by men like Ames and Keener who had personally transformed the arguments for the case method in the 1880s, and thus had been aware of the extent to which these were rationalizations. But by 1920 Ames and Keener were dead, and most law teachers had become acquainted with the case method in their student days after it was fully transformed. For them, it seemingly had always been there, in place and inevitable. While Ames had been intensely committed to the survival of the case method because his career as a teacher and a scholar turned on it, only with the second generation of case-method teachers did there arise a partiality approaching faith. For instance, while Freund's 1902 curriculum seemed "heretical" to both Ames and Beale, it caused Ames to be more deeply "disturbed" and "anxious."[34]

The phenomenon of a growing skepticism toward Harvard as the proper model for legal education accompanied by a deepening commitment to Harvard's essential method can be demonstrated most clearly in the career of Thomas Reed Powell, one of the twentieth century's eminent public law scholars, whom Freund hoped to recruit for the Commonwealth Fund inquiry. Earlier than most, Powell had reacted against the view that the outcomes of cases turn primarily upon the search for controlling principles enunciated in previously decided cases. This was the view of Langdell and Ames, although by no means original with them, and it pervaded the Harvard Law School classroom at the turn of the century. When Powell graduated from the Law School in 1904, he had "the impression that somehow or other the eternal principles

34. See p. 55, above.

of the common law were encased in the Year Books. . . . It never occurred to me that we could aim at a goal and get there. . . . Two years later I took graduate work at Columbia and soon came to call the process one of getting de-Harvardized." At Columbia, where he began to work for a Ph.D. in the School of Political Science, Powell encountered professors who were "on to the judging game." Especially there was Goodnow, "a poor lawyer according to standards I had been brought up to at Harvard, but he looked first toward his end and then made for it. I couldn't escape seeing from him how courts actually behaved in public law."[35] Thus, Powell felt that he had been "de-Harvardized," as if the older view of the objective reality and controlling effect of legal rules was peculiar to the Harvard Law School or represented Harvard's principal contribution to legal education.

In any event, for the next half-dozen years Powell studied public law from the de-Harvardized perspective of political science. He was an instructor at Columbia in 1907, then at Illinois from 1908 to 1910. Returning to Columbia in 1911, he began working his way up in the faculty of political science. Writing extensively on administration, he received his Ph.D. in 1913, and from 1913 to 1916 he served as the managing editor of the *Political Science Quarterly* in addition to teaching.[36]

Truly, Powell's seemed to be a de-Harvardized career. But even before he had finished his stint at the *Political Science Quarterly*, Powell—however much he thought himself de-Harvardized—had begun to reenter the intellectual orbit of the Harvard Law School. He had begun to give the instruction in constitutional law at the Columbia Law School and to be caught up once again with the experience of the case class, this time from the teacher's side. By the end of the decade, Powell was oriented mainly toward his law school duties, and

35. Powell to Jerome Frank, November 5, 1930, Powell MSS, box A-5, Harvard Law School Library.

36. R. Gordon Hoxie et al., *A History of the Faculty of Political Science, Columbia University* (New York: Columbia University Press, 1955), 268.

in 1925 he returned to the Harvard Law School to teach constitutional law there. Of course, to Powell's mind his law classes were "de-Harvardized," that is, free from an obsession with locating controlling principles in the cases under discussion, and at the Harvard of the twenties this made Powell a bit of a maverick. As he wrote to Jerome Frank in 1930, "of late years the third-year men have been pretty well on to Beale and Ed Warren. Yet the passion for a pillow still prevails. I can still recall the shock I caused two years ago by telling the obvious distinction between two cases after vainly getting the students to tell it: one was decided one way; and the other, the other. To let it go at that seemed impious to them."[37]

But, having reentered the intellectual milieu of the case method, Powell's impiety had its limits. When Freund asked Powell to join him in the work of the Commonwealth Fund on administration, Powell declined. "The more I think about it," he replied, "the more persuaded I am that I am not suited to any of the work which you have in mind . . . so much of [the] work is alien to my aptitude and present interest."[38] The problem, according to Freund, was "that Powell will work only on judicial decisions."[39]

What was so compelling about the study of cases for a man like Powell who scorned intellectual pillows? It was the same thing that caused him to return to a law school and teach cases. Cases, and not other sources, were the business of the legal scholar and the law school, and that should be obvious. "It seems, sometimes, that many of the criticisms, expressed or implied, which are made of legal education reduce themselves to the objection that the law school teaches law." It seemed to Powell that "if the law school is to remain a law school, the subject matter with which it is to deal is neces-

37. Powell to Frank, November 5, 1930, Powell MSS, box A-5 (quotation); Hoxie, *Faculty of Political Science*, 268.

38. Powell to Ernst Freund, n.d., Freund MSS, box 2 addenda, "Commonwealth Fund," University of Chicago Library.

39. Draft letter to Max Farrand, n.d., ibid.

sarily fixed by the content and the structure of the law."[40] When Powell had studied under Goodnow, he had studied public administration and political science; now that he was again at a law school, he obviously studied and taught law. He associated "law" almost entirely with the work of the regular courts, and in this regard Powell was no more de-Harvardized than Langdell or Ames.

This association was supported and reinforced for Powell by the constant experience of the case class. It told him that a law school was the place for a superior intellect to be. The case ritual was hard and demanding, and those who mastered it could be trusted to know what law was. Ames had seen that only the cleverest men in the Harvard Law School were fit for it. Powell, who had explored beyond the law school walls, saw that really only the cleverest men in the whole university were fit for it. "My impression in the days at Columbia when I knew graduate students was that for the most part people who went into the field of administration were the inferior men intellectually."[41] They could not have withstood the case class. Indeed, what graduate student in any field of the arts and sciences could? Even the law student, once severed from the constant interrogation, withered intellectually. "My work as a student and teacher of Constitutional Law has directed my attention particularly to the attitude of lawyers towards the constitutionality of legislation. . . . I hear the nouns 'liberty,' 'freedom,' 'justice,' 'equality,' interpreted in the light of airy metaphysical fancy in pitiful disregard of obvious fact. . . . And I wonder at the reason. I wonder why men feel so strongly that they seem to lose the capacity to think."[42]

Because the case ritual was hard, because it broke down and built up and broke down again the assumptions of the

40. Thomas Reed Powell, "Law as a University Study," *Columbia University Quarterly*, 19 (1917): 117, 118–19.

41. Powell to M. T. Van Hecke, November 21, 1934, Powell MSS, box A-6; with regard to Ames, see p. 34, above.

42. Thomas Reed Powell, "Law as a Cultural Study," American Bar Association, *Reports*, 42 (1917); 576–77.

student on the topic under discussion, Powell like many second-generation teachers had come to the belief that the schools that practiced it "emphasize above everything else the development of the power to think."[43] It did not so much matter what one thought about—that day after day it was only the adjudication of the regular courts; what was important was that the case class seemed to be the supreme test of mental alertness. Those who had mastered it completely could be relied upon to know what was law and what was not. For Powell and the second generation, no mere belief, no unexamined assumption, no intellectual pillow could survive the remorseless testing of the case method.[44]

As Ames had declared at the moment of victory in 1903, the time for dealing with the relative merits of the case method had passed.[45] This shift in emphasis compounded the difficulties of scholarship such as Freund's, with its implied criticism of the case method, for the true believer simply filtered out whatever his faith told him he should not hear. For instance, in his reaction to the Redlich Report in 1915, Harlan F. Stone had declared that it "confirms the opinion which most of us had formed, that the case method is the scientific method of instruction in the common law." As a result of Professor Redlich's efforts, it "will not be surprising, therefore, to find American law teachers by the case method reluctant to engage in any experimental tinkering with a system which on the whole works well and inspires student and teacher alike with an extraordinary intellectual enthusiasm."[46] Stone was not being disingenuous, but simply acknowledging Redlich's willingness to admit that the case method had its uses. As regards Redlich's suggestion that the case-method curriculum needed to impart a more comprehensive view of the law, Stone knew

43. Powell, "University Study," 111.

44. The continuation of this syndrome down to the present will be discussed at chap. 5, sec. 4, below.

45. See p. 59, above.

46. Remarks of Dean H. F. Stone, in "Papers and Discussion Concerning the Redlich Report," *American Law School Review*, 4 (1916): 92.

that law students were already receiving the truest sense of what law was simply by being exposed to the process of studying cases. After all, the whole point of the case method, as transformers like John Chipman Gray had seen more clearly than the teachers of the second generation, was that it was not simply a skill-honing device, but a medium for perpetuating a sense of what the law was; a sense, more precisely, of the common law "as a living thing. . . . We desire that the students may be filled with its spirit." Against this spirit, Redlich's arguments had no chance.[47]

Nor would Freund's in the 1920s. As the decade advanced, it became clear that his hopes for the Commonwealth Fund inquiry and his survey would not be realized. While law teachers acknowledged him as a leading authority in his field, they did so primarily on the basis of his administrative law casebook, issued originally in 1911, and on the resulting perception of him as a narrow technician concerned with appealing administrative decisions to the regular courts. But his survey works, *Administrative Powers*, appearing in 1928, and *Legislative Regulation*, in 1932, were not widely read, and even if they had been, their perspectives would probably have been beyond the comprehension of most American law teachers. According to a former student, Freund "once wistfully confessed that he had never read an understanding review of one of his books."[48] Even the casebook, where he had taken pains in his introduction to indicate that the concerns of legal scholarship should be broader than those which occupied the courts on review, only served to reinforce the judicentric viewpoints of the teachers who used it. Once, while attempting to demonstrate the importance of teaching a statutes course in a law school, Freund was unable to keep himself from remarking on the futility of the effort. While such a course was feasible, he said, the "danger is that with the usual training of law teachers, they would almost inevitably be

47. J. C. Gray, "Methods of Legal Education—IV," *Yale Law Journal*, 1 (1892): 159, 156; also see p. 40, above.

48. Maurice T. Van Hecke, "Ernst Freund as a Teacher of Legislation," *University of Chicago Law Review*, 1 (1933): 92.

drawn to the constitutional problems . . . which they could handle on the basis of cases. In the hands of most teachers the course would tend to become a course in *Constitutional Law*."[49] All things, it was clear, had to begin and end with the courts and their cases.[50]

3

If Frankfurter's approach to administrative government seemed so reasonable as to be almost self-evident in the world of legal education, the same was true in the larger world. Freund might wish to center the study of administration in law schools, to make it a part of the law. But in the world of the 1920s, such a degree of connection between law and administration seemed scarcely plausible. Rather, the study of administrative behavior was undeniably the province of the "science" of public administration and of its academic cousin, political science. With proprietary indignation, public administrationists and political scientists railed against the law's meddlesome procedural requirements and against the judicial review of administrative decisions.[51] Indeed, it almost seemed

49. Ernst Freund, "Memorandum to Serve as a Basis for a Round Table Discussion on a Course in Statutes," *North Carolina Law Review*, 1 (1922): 106.

50. Ernst Freund, *Cases on Administrative Law* (St. Paul: West Publishing Co., 1911), ix, 1–3; and second edition of same (1928), v–vi; Freund, "Administrative Law," *Encyclopaedia of the Social Sciences* (New York: Macmillan, 1930), 1:454–55; Patterson, *Jurisprudence*, 90; Maurice H. Merrill, "Three Possible Approaches to the Study of Administrative Law," *Iowa Law Review*, 18 (1933): 228; Oliver P. Field, "Study of Administrative Law," 234–35. Perhaps the most intriguing misperception of Freund was Felix Frankfurter's in a posthumous tribute. It turns history on its head: "And, while in the beginning, for him, administrative law was the control of administrative agencies by the courts, he came soon to see that administrative law also described the controls exercised by the administrative agencies." Quoted in Oscar Krains, *The World and Ideas of Ernst Freund* (University, Ala.: University of Alabama Press, 1974), at p. 153.

51. John H. Gray and Jack Levin, *The Valuation of Public Utilities* (New York: Harper, 1933), 118–20; Dwight Waldo, *The Administrative State* (New York: Ronald Press, 1948), 79.

as if "the arm of the law . . . reached into the . . . management of public affairs from the outside, like a cold pike."[52]

This was more than a happy coincidence for Frankfurter's interests, however. Thirty years earlier, public administration as a discipline had been nonexistent, political science was in a crude infancy, and the study of administration, such as it was, was almost wholly a part of public law. But for the law's forebearance, "public administration" would have remained at the level of its sources: political science, scientific management theory, the city manager movement, and the work of municipal research bureaus. That is, by the 1920s, it may have described some tools of rational management in governmental affairs, but there would have been little occasion for it to describe comprehensively the behavior, and especially the decision-making, of regulatory commissioners. Instead, this concern would have been in large part a province of the law.[53] That is what non–case-method scholars like Goodnow and Freund had been working for in the 1890s. But Goodnow had become frustrated with affairs at Columbia, and Freund had been prevented from building an institutional base for the study of public law at Chicago.[54]

52. Fritz Morstein Marx, "Administrative Regulation in Comparative Perspective," *Law and Contemporary Problems*, 26 (1961): 319.

53. Glendon Schubert, "The Future of Public Law," *George Washington Law Review*, 34 (1966): 593–608; Barry Dean Karl, *Executive Reorganization and Reform in the New Deal: The Genesis of Administrative Management, 1900–1939* (Cambridge: Harvard University Press, 1963), 115–27, 264; Marx, "Administrative Regulation," 307–28; Waldo, *Administrative State*, 16–61.

54. See pp. 48–50, 52–58, above. In this regard, see James Barr Ames to Charles W. Eliot, August 1, 1900, Eliot Papers, box 100, folder 4, Harvard University Archives. In response to Eliot's proposal to enlarge the Harvard Law School curriculum so as to prepare the students for service in the higher grades of the public service, Ames replied that there could be ". . . little in common between the present Law Faculty and the new teachers, and also very little cooperation between the two classes of students. I am sure our Faculty would not wish the new professors to have a voice in shaping the curriculum leading to the degree of LL.B., and I doubt if they would take much interest in the curriculum leading to the degree in Political Science." Elsewhere in the letter Ames implies that only private law (con-

By the 1920s, consequently, a "science" of public administration had arisen that worked hand-in-glove with Frankfurter's desire that lawyers not inquire too closely into the work of administration. Its "fundamental principles" laid out the working environment of the expert—one that was wholly rational and inspired, and sealed against contamination by political influence, legalism, or "mere" bureaucracy. The expert in a commission pursued the public interest much as the scientist in a laboratory pursued the immutable laws of physical existence; and in the same steady way that the physical sciences expand their boundaries, so was society to progress and prosper. If, in everyday reality, the commissions of the early twentieth century seemed not to have attained this regime of expertise, one could almost believe upon reading the literature of public administration that the shortfall was due only to some correctable leakage into the expert's environment of political influence and other contaminants.[55]

Indeed, this belief had become so pervasive that discoveries of a contrary administrative reality, such as the Thompson Committee's in New York,[56] no longer posed a real threat. What Ames had said of the Harvard model of legal education in 1903 could now be said of the approach to administrative law and government designed to preserve that model: the battle was fought and the time for speaking to the merits had passed. Thus, in New York, the Thompson Committee plan was not enacted into law. It was defeated principally because its authors were thought to be politically motivated and only

---

tracts, real property, sales, and the like) can be properly thought of as law, that anything else is "political science" ("the student of Political Science would not wisely concern himself with Private Law. . . . the new 'annex' to the Law School . . . would, as I believe, add very little, if anything, to the prestige of the School").

55. Frederick C. Mosher, *Democracy and the Public Service* (New York: Oxford University Press, 1968), 70–83; see generally, William H. Allen, *Efficient Democracy* (New York: Dodd, Mead, 1907); Luther Gulick et al., *Papers on the Science of Public Administration*, ed. Luther Gulick and L. Urwick (New York: Institute of Public Administration, 1937).

56. See latter part of chap. 3, sec. 1, above.

superficially interested in the problem of regulation. In the legislature and among the public, the provision for a judicial approach was derided when it was not ignored. The Committee majority was Republican, and it was assumed that the Republicans, who had returned to power after several years of Tammany rule, were merely looking for a way to embarrass the Tammany-dominated Commission.[57]

Significantly, the Committee minority did not share this view. But by 1920, New Yorkers at large simply had lost the capacity to redefine the proposition of governmental regulation and to propose a departure such as the Second District Commission had been in 1907. In 1907, for instance, there had been widespread dissatisfaction with governmental regulation, and it was hoped that the Commission would work an improvement. By 1920, there was widespread dissatisfaction with the Commission's regulation, but it was generally agreed that no new device need be sought, for the Commission's expertise had only fallen temporary victim to maladies not of its making. The proper form of regulation was thought to have been found, at least in theory, and anyone who proposed a departure more drastic than the reinvigorating of expertise did not meet with success. Citizens dissatisfied with the service and rates of public service companies and frustrated with the equivocations of the Public Service Commission demanded action from their elected representatives. But what they generally received were promises to look into the matter of raising the quality of Commission personnel.[58]

Given that scholarly opinion had shut the door on alternate responses, this tenacity with which ordinary New Yorkers

57. Delos F. Wilcox, "The Crisis in Public Service Regulation in New York," *National Municipal Review*, 4 (1915): 558–63; *New York Times*, March 10, 1915, p. 12; ibid., March 13, 1915, p. 12; ibid., May 27, 1915, p. 10; Martin Landau, "The New York Public Service Commission, 1907–1930" (Ph.D. diss., New York University, 1952), 60–85.

58. Landau, "New York Public Service Commission," 75–84; Blake McKelvey, *Rochester: The Quest for Quality, 1890–1925* (Cambridge: Harvard University Press, 1956), 340; Joint Legislative Committee to Investigate the Public Service Commissions, *Complete Report* (Albany: J. B. Lyon Company, 1917), 3–12, 206–26, 281.

clung to the notion of Commission expertise is understandable. It arose in good measure from what was viewed as the only plausible alternative to Commission regulation. This was to admit that there was no means of bringing harmony to a disorderly society. If there were not experts, it seemed, then there would be warfare. According to one observer, the "expressions 'traction war,' 'gas fight,' 'telephone controversy,' 'electric light dispute,' etc., are familiar to everyone. In the picturesque language of the newspaper and the street, public service corporations have long been described as public enemies, and the attitude of belligerency toward them has become chronic in many, if not most, American cities."[59] As long as one could hope that there was such a thing as administrative expertise and that the Commission had been beset by "Tammanyization" only temporarily, it seemed frightful that regulation should become a battleground. It seemed better to refer the potential combatants to the administrative process and hope that the experts could effect a truce.[60]

To seal the matter, this popular opinion was reinforced by the "public opinion of the bar."[61] The Thompson Committee was composed of lawyers, of course, but within the profession it was a voice crying in the wilderness. More representative of professional opinion was, for instance, the debate on the nature of commission government that had been held in the New York Constitutional Convention of 1915. The standing of the Committee lawyers was relatively humble in comparison to that of the Convention lawyers, whose number included Elihu Root and a recent attorney general of the United States, George Wickersham. For the former group, the question of the judicial function was a commonsense proposition, to be

59. Delos F. Wilcox, "Fundamental Planks in a Public Utility Program," American Academy of Political and Social Science, *Annals*, 57 (1915): 8.

60. G. Edward White, "The Social Values of the Progressives: Some New Perspectives," *South Atlantic Quarterly*, 70 (1971): 72, 76; Thomas K. McCraw, "The Progressive Legacy," in Lewis F. Gould, ed., *The Progressive Era* (Syracuse University Press, 1974), 182, 189, 199.

61. Elihu Root, "The Layman's Criticism of the Lawyer," American Bar Association, *Reports*, 39 (1914): 391; see p. 17, above.

resolved from their experience. If a body had a judicial function, it should be held to the standards of performance imposed on the courts. For the lawyers of the Convention, however, the question required more esoteric reference—to legal literature. The precise formulation of the nature of commission government adopted by the Convention was Wickersham's:

> The commissions are clothed with certain powers; without specifying them we understand in general what they are. They are partially legislative and they are partially executive. Of course, they act in a judicial manner. Under some of the decisions of the Court of Appeals in this State, they act judicially and exercise judicial powers. Of course, this is wholly a violation of the correct legal interpretation of the idea of the commissions.[62]

What is striking about Wickersham's statement is that it was no clearer or more confused than other statements made about the administrative power by lawyers in the three decades since the creation of the Interstate Commerce Commission in 1887. The legal issues of administrative government had presented themselves for analysis during this period, but guided by the "correct legal interpretation" arising from the universities, the profession as a whole had made little advance in understanding.

Against the opinion-makers of the bar, the experiences of the Stevens era and of the Thompson Committee investigation counted for very little. Rather, to the lawyer's eye, as guided by the legal scholar, there were a number of glaring defects in any approach such as that proposed by the Thompson Committee. For one thing, the scope of review was too broad. A reviewing court in orthodox theory could reverse or remand an administrative decision only for errors of law, or for determinative findings of fact which were not supported by "substantial" evidence from the hearing record. According to this substantial evidence rule, as long as the court could find

62. *Record of the Constitutional Convention 1915* (Albany: J. B. Lyon Company, 1915), 2:2171.

that some evidence in the record supported the administrative finding (the testimony of one witness, for instance), and even though the preponderance of the evidence was contrary (the testimony of fifty other witnesses), the court had to affirm. Any other result, it was said, would vitiate the administrative process by permitting the retrying of administrative controversies in the regular courts.[63]

This conclusion was based on an assumption that administrative decisions were informed by expertise and therefore deserved the respect of nonexpert courts. But, as the Thompson Committee discovered in the course of its investigation, administrative decisions could very likely be the products of a "Tammanyized" commission.[64] In such instances, the kind of review that seemed to be required was one that was at least as thorough as that which a "Tammany" commissioner had experienced during his prior service as a trial court judge. The question for the Thompson Committee was not whether it should permit a doubtful expertise to soar to the heights of orthodox fancy, but whether it could provide some reasonable expectation of getting a little more precise performance from severely earthbound administrators.[65] Yet in orthodox theory the Committee's reliance on a disciplined process of adjudication was fatal.

The Thompson Committee would have ousted an open-ended expertise from its policy-making role, of course, but in orthodox theory the problem of policy-making through adjudication was thought to be more complex than that. The role of an administrative agency was to enforce and elaborate upon the legislature's statutory decision that certain areas of society be regulated in a certain broad way. The agency was conceived to be an extension of the legislature, and therefore its elaboration of legislative policy ought to be done quasi-legislatively—that is, by promulgating regulations that would ex-

63. Bernard Schwartz, *Administrative Law* (Boston: Little, Brown, 1976), 589–95.

64. See latter part of chap. 3, sec. 1, above.

65. Joint Legislative Committee, *Complete Report*, 118–20, 156–57; and see latter part of chap. 3, sec. 1, above.

pand upon the general wording of the enabling statute. The reason that the agency had been given quasi-judicial authority to adjudicate controversies arising under the statute and its own regulations was primarily to accelerate and strengthen the process of regulation by avoiding the reputedly slow and biased enforcement proceedings of the regular courts. Adjudication in the administrative context was thought to be primarily an enforcement device, and the "law" that was applied to the contested fact situations of an administrative trial was supposed to be preexisting policy enunciated in agency regulations.

Naturally, orthodox theory provided for the possibility that a certain number of adjudications would present novel situations not covered by existing agency regulations. Here administrative expertise would have to devise a rule for the case, with the result that a losing party would be judged by a "law" not promulgated at the time his dispute arose. This retroactive effect was unavoidable in policy-making by adjudication, and thus just and efficient administration was said to require that it be kept to a minimum.[66]

With regard to this abstract justice of administrative policy-making, orthodox theory may indeed have had the better case. But practically, the Thompson Committee had seen in two years of investigation that quasi-legislative policy-making was so difficult as to be next to impossible. Attempting to act quasi-legislatively, the administrative policy-maker experienced the same distress that had moved the legislature to delegate policy-making authority to him in the first place. In a pluralistic society, the enunciation of policy in other than vague and equivocal terms was politically hazardous to the legislator, be he an elected representative or an administrative delegate. Of course, in orthodox theory the continuous supervision of regulatory problems by the administrative quasi-legislator was supposed to give rise to an expertise that the parent legislature could not call upon. This expertise was

66. A. A. Berle, "The Expansion of American Administrative Law," *Harvard Law Review*, 30 (1917): 430–48.

supposed to enable the administrator to define precisely a transcendent "public interest" underlying his policies to which all the interest groups and interested minorities in American society would reflexively yield.[67] But in two years of searching, the Thompson Committee had failed to find any examples of this dynamic.[68]

Indeed, what the Thompson Committee had found was that, realistically, the safest course for the administrator was to seek "judicial" sanctuary. He took refuge almost exclusively in the adjudicatory process, invoking the symbols of judicial office when declarations of his expertise were insufficient to protect him from the conflicting demands of the various interest groups that he was supposed to regulate. A posture of "even-handedness" was assumed which purported to extend the legal requirement of procedural fairness into the area of substantive decision-making and to require that the outcome of cases be "balanced." A decision that appeased the litigants, mainly by splitting the difference in the issues of their dispute, was said to be balanced, fair, and judicial.[69] This approach was quite opposed to Stevens' sense of judicial decision-making, where "fairness . . . did not mean giving one party half of its demands, but instead, consisted of listening to arguments of both sides and then making decisions irrespective of who the parties were."[70]

Given that the administrative process seemed to have been driven almost inevitably to a judicial posture of some sort by the pluralistic nature of American society, the experience of the Second District Commission suggested to the Thompson Committee that there was something to be gained in pushing

67. Grant McConnell, *Private Power and American Democracy* (New York: Knopf, 1966), 30–50; more generally, Glendon Schubert, *The Public Interest* (Glencoe, Ill.: Free Press, 1960).

68. Joint Legislative Committee, *Complete Report*, 118–19, 156.

69. Ibid., 118; William E. Mosher and Finla G. Crawford, *Public Utility Regulation* (New York: Harper, 1933), 34–39.

70. Remarks of Chairman Stevens, "Thursday Evening Session," *Electric Railway Journal*, 41 (1913): 424.

beyond judicial form and into its substance.[71] A fully developed judicial approach both compelled the making of clearly defined policy and protected it more completely than the charade of "judicialization." To be sure, the policy which was produced and protected was more retroactive in its effect upon litigants and more slow and plodding in its development than the lightning thrusts of order envisioned for the regime of expertise in orthodox theory, but it was policy nonetheless.[72]

Yet even if these perspectives had penetrated professional thinking in the 1920s, there was still a final obstacle. This was the courts. Encouraged by legal scholarship, they had sanctioned the finality of administrative decisions almost from the beginning of the modern administrative process in 1887, and by the 1920s, a systematic review on the merits would have created a caseload of unmanageable proportions. What might have occasioned an evolutionary expansion of the appellate system in 1887 now augured an institution-threatening flood of new litigation. Accordingly, the judges of the appellate courts ordinarily treated administrative decisions as final, while attempting on occasion to reverse the worst instances of administrative decision-making on the pretext of some violation of procedural due process.[73]

Such forebearance, of course, is not the accepted impression of the stance of the courts toward the administrative process in this period. But if, in an era of substantive due process, the courts placed limits on government in general that were perhaps too restrictive for the needs of society, the field of administrative discretion within those limits was still

71. Joint Legislative Committee, *Complete Report*, 120–65.

72. I might reiterate here a point I have made before and will make again: that an administrative experience of this sort should also have provided lessons for the policy-making of regular court judges in the 1980s; see pp. 3–5, 77–83, above, and 160, below.

73. John Dickinson, *Administrative Justice and the Supremacy of Law in the United States* (Cambridge: Harvard University Press, 1927), 39–75, 157–235.

vast; and one need only look to the history of an American administrative agency to see how unguided by judicial discipline that discretion was on most questions coming before the administrative process. The same court, for example, that handed down the *Lochner* decision began the line of decisions that stripped the federal judiciary of the potential for reviewing the substance of administrative decisions on a systematic basis. With the noisy and ill-advised exception of rates, reviewing courts were disposed to characterize administrative decisions arrived at by means of a primitive judicialism as the products of an expertise beyond the comprehension of nonexpert appellate judges.[74]

4

By the late 1920s, then, it could no longer be doubted that the future of administrative law and government would be the one envisioned by Felix Frankfurter: that of legal forebearance, of confining a judicial approach to the form of administration and not its substance, of leaving the administrative process to feel its way by means of trial and error, with the conviction that the end result of all this would be a successful step in the evolution of the American Republic.

What degree of success might in fact be attained, Ernst Freund ventured to guess toward the end of his life. The following passage, written in 1928, is perhaps the most powerful in all the literature of American administration, for it anticipates by fifty years conclusions about the administrative process that have been taken to be the intellectual breakthroughs of the late twentieth century:

> It has been shown that this [administrative] discretion represents a trial-and-error method of evolving standards, assuming that standards can ultimately be evolved. If this assumption is untrue, the

74. George F. Dix, "The Death of the Commerce Court: A Study in Institutional Weakness," *American Journal of Legal History*, 8 (1964): 238–60; Robert B. Highsaw, *Edward Douglass White* (Baton Rouge: Louisiana State University Press, 1981): 98–100; John Bauer, *Transforming Public Utility Regulation* (New York: Harper, 1950), 30–49.

quasi-judicial administrative process involves a fallacy; and theoretically it may be said that it would be more straightforward to have regulation take the more arbitrary form of a legislative fiat, or of determinations by boards frankly constituted on the basis of interest representation. . . . But it may be that there is no objective standard, and yet that the demonstration of this may be too protracted to count practically, i.e., the trial-and-error method may be continued indefinitely, all the parties deluding themselves that they are engaged, if not in a scientific process, at least in its formative "stages."[75]

A rather bleak assessment, yet Freund continued to write, if only for himself. "I think it is the younger men who should take the initiative; but I should be very willing to give you the benefit of my experience; I have definite ideas, if nothing else."[76]

75. Ernst Freund, *Administrative Powers over Persons and Property* (Chicago: University of Chicago Press, 1928), 583; compare Louis L. Jaffe, "The Illusion of the Ideal Administration," *Harvard Law Review*, 86 (1973): 1197–98; Charles A. Reich, "The Law of the Planned Society," *Yale Law Journal*, 75 (1966): 1233–38; Richard B. Stewart, "The Reformation of American Administrative Law," *Harvard Law Review*, 88 (1975): 1667–1813.

76. Freund to Robert B. Mathews, October 21, 1929, Freund MSS, box 11, "Statutes."

5

The Fruits of Avoidance, 1932 to the Present

1

December 11, 1932, was a forbidding day in Chicago, with wind and snow blowing wildly. At the University of Chicago that afternoon a memorial service was held in the campus chapel for Ernst Freund, who had died earlier in the autumn. The tributes of those who braved the day to attend were the conventional expressions of regard for a departed friend and colleague, and reading what was said of Freund on this occasion by those who had known him in life, one is not surprised that half a century after his death his name is all but forgotten.[1]

This obscurity, however, does not measure the man so much as the resolve of those who opposed his approach to administration. For over forty years, Freund had sought to make its study one of the important undertakings of American legal scholarship, and twice—in 1902 and during the early 1920s—he had been on the verge of success. Each time, however, his efforts had been repelled at the last moment by case-method scholars, with the result that by the beginning of the New Deal legal science was little better qualified to analyze the ways and means of administrative power than it had been at the turn of the century.

Seen with both the hindsight of history and the foresight of Freund's published works, this was an unnecessary result, and it was one that was to contribute in no small measure to the problems of administrative government and the quandaries of

1. *University* [of Chicago] *Record*, 19 (1933): 39–47.

administrative law down to the present day. Before the New Deal, Freund anticipated almost every fundamental analysis of the administrative process that has been offered by legal scholars since then, and it is indicative of the completeness of his defeat by those who opposed him during his career that he is remembered today only as an obscure professor whose "concept of administration seems . . . very ill-conceived. . . . it would make modern government impossible and would deprive us of many fruitful solutions."[2]

But it was not modern government that Freund threatened. It was the fabric of careers dependent upon the university law school as it existed at the beginning of this century. The story of the contribution of legal scholarship to the evolution of administrative government had been one of the emergence and triumph of a scholarship of avoidance, and to this end the defeat of Ernst Freund had been essential. With his death, the course was set.

2

According to one of his students, speaking on the eve of the New Deal, Felix Frankfurter's administrative law seminar at the Harvard Law School was stimulating because it conveyed "an attitude, a way of looking at things, rather than specific information. The feeling which one obtains . . . may be likened to that with which one looks out over the Great Plains from some peak of the Rockies. There is the same sense of an illimitable vista, of broadened perception, of realization of the unity of the domain surveyed, of inspiration and uplift."[3]

Along with his work as a publicist and his direction of the Commonwealth Fund's field studies, Frankfurter's seminar was a principal source of his influence. With the tremendous expansion of the administrative process during the New Deal,

2. Louis L. Jaffe, "The Illusion of the Ideal Administration," *Harvard Law Review*, 86 (1973): 1186.

3. Maurice H. Merrill, "Three Possible Approaches to the Study of Administrative Law," *Iowa Law Review*, 18 (1933): 230–31.

Frankfurter's seminar students would find employment as members of agencies, as consultants to government on questions of administrative law and practice, and as teachers and writers in the field.[4] During this decade, they would venture down from the peaks of administration into its valleys, where the judges and practitioners labored, in order to lead the profession around swamps of "premature synthesis"[5] and other dangers. They would be convinced that the New Deal was not the culmination of a half century's evolution, primarily in the direction of avoidance, but only the dawn of the "formative years." They would respond with "exuberant optimism" to the expansion of the administrative process and would counter skepticism about its expertise with "a celebration, a defense, and a rationalization of the magnificent accomplishment."[6] It was to be a case, as Frankfurter liked to say, of "the law is what the lawyers are" and "the law and the lawyers are what the law schools make them."[7] The "naivete . . . which . . . assumes that the qualities of all the young Harvard Law

4. H. N. Hirsch, *The Enigma of Felix Frankfurter* (New York: Basic Books, 1981), 99–111; Frankfurter's compulsive need for protégés and influence is analyzed at pp. 206–9, ibid.; Donald A. Ritchie, *James M. Landis* (Cambridge: Harvard University Press, 1980), 21, 32–34, 45–46; some of the Commonwealth Fund studies evolved out of student work in Frankfurter's seminar, such as Edwin Wilhite Patterson, *The Insurance Commissioner in the United States* (Cambridge: Harvard University Press, 1927); see ibid., vii–viii; but Frankfurter's triumph in this area was his masterminding of the economist I. L. Sharfman's massive and highly influential celebration of expertise, *The Interstate Commerce Commission* (New York: The Commonwealth Fund, 1931–37); see ibid., vol. 1, p. x; vol. 4, conclusion.

5. Paraphrase of Felix Frankfurter, review of Ernst Freund et al., *The Growth of American Administrative Law* (1923), in *Harvard Law Review*, 37 (1924): 640; see p. 106, above.

6. Louis L. Jaffe, "James Landis and the Administrative Process," *Harvard Law Review*, 78 (1964): 319, 320.

7. Quoted in Jerold S. Auerbach, *Unequal Justice* (New York: Oxford University Press, 1976), 149. I think that it is safe to say that this theme runs throughout Frankfurter's correspondence and writings, and, if H. N. Hirsch is correct in his psychological interpretation of Frankfurter, it is not difficult to see why it would; see chap. 4, n. 5, and chap. 5, n. 4, above.

School lawyers in Washington were really unaffected by their training in the Harvard Law School is too innocent."[8]

Thus, during the 1930s, the legal scholar became a participant in government, whereas before he had influenced government primarily through his writings. James Landis, Louis Jaffe, Charles Wyzanski, and scores of other academic lawyers joined, in Jaffe's words, "a whole phalanx of talented, passionate . . . men" who helped to bring "the New Deal legislation into being and stoked the high fires of its administration."[9]

If Frankfurter was the general of this phalanx, James Landis was the captain of its front line, and indeed by the end of the decade, after Frankfurter had gone to the Supreme Court and Landis had published his lectures on the administrative process,[10] Landis emerged as the chief spokesman for the Harvard approach. He epitomized the beliefs, the enthusiasms, and the talents of those scholarly lawyers who were a generation younger than Frankfurter and who carried Frankfurter's views into practice during the New Deal. According to Louis Jaffe, "Landis spoke for all of us who had been intimately associated with the administrative process."[11]

Like his fellow scholars in government, Landis' mood "was one of exuberant optimism,"[12] and only fleetingly did he glimpse that this might rest upon a simplistic estimate of the problems to be found in administrative government—problems which had been avoided for half a century by the Harvard approach. He saw well enough the ill preparation of his

8. Frankfurter to Thomas Reed Powell, December 18, 1933, Powell MSS, box A-6, Harvard Law School Library; Frankfurter was discussing Jerome Frank's criticism of legal education as ill preparation for the realities of law practice. ("Jerry Frank is a sweet fellow, but he does write balderdash about legal education. . . . He is a sweet child.")

9. Jaffe, "Landis," 323.

10. James M. Landis, *The Administrative Process* (New Haven: Yale University Press, 1938).

11. Jaffe, "Landis," 320. However, Landis' personal relationship with Frankfurter grew temporarily strained in the mid-1930s; see Ritchie, *Landis*, 64, 67–68, 81, 89.

12. Jaffe, "Landis," 319.

fellow law teachers for their governmental responsibilities, but it seemed to make little impression on him. Thus, he knew that "the traditional methods of instruction centering on the solution of the individual case have the defect of tending to obscure institutional consideration. . . . Institutional criticism . . . is only less a subject of consideration in the law schools than at the bar."[13] He saw, moreover, the "lack of knowledge concerning" administration. "How rarely the subject has been the continuing concern of our law schools is illustrated by the fact that today [1940] of the eighty teachers of the subject, only 8 or 10% have lived with it for more than a period of ten years."[14] But he believed that the cure for this was simply to be involved with the administration of the New Deal.

There, in the words of Louis Jaffe, one felt "the unique concatenation of circumstances" that gave impetus to the administrative process under the New Deal: "the desperate panic of the people; the terrible shock to the confidence and prestige of those who had held power; the rush into the vacuum of . . . exasperated, deprived men, those who for years had been clamoring for reform. . . . These men had ready an enormous, articulated backlog of tasks long overdue, tasks pent up, waiting to be achieved."[15] If, in later years, it was "too easy . . . to see that the normal, everyday potential of the administrative process" could not draw upon these forces, "[w]e must recall . . . that our generation—that of Landis and myself—judged the administrative process in terms of its stunning performance under the New Deal."[16]

As the "social service state appeared to [rise] as a full-

13. James M. Landis, "The Study of Legislation in Law Schools," *Harvard Graduates' Magazine*, 39 (1931): 435.

14. James M. Landis, "Crucial Issues in Administrative Law," *Harvard Law Review*, 53 (1940): 1078.

15. Jaffe, "Landis," 323.

16. Ibid.; apparently to arrive at "stunning," they discounted personal experiences that ran counter to their belief in expertise; see Michael E. Parrish, *Securities Regulation and the New Deal* (New Haven: Yale University

fledged phoenix from the ashes of the Great Depression,"[17] the complexities and nagging doubts that Ernst Freund had expressed about the administrative process seemed not to exist for the New Deal lawyers. Their truth, as Edward S. Corwin observed, was the "desirability of supporting government power as a general proposition."[18] Thus, only a year or two after his death, Freund's works disappear from scholarly discussions of administration except as footnotes, and even these fade as the decade progresses. By 1940, it could appear to Landis that "until 1930 students of the subject were few and far between, the literature was scanty and generally poor in quality."[19] For him as well as the other young lawyers of the New Deal, there was almost nothing to learn from the half century of administrative history that preceded their efforts.[20]

Based upon their experiences in the 1930s, the scholarly lawyers of the New Deal were convinced of one thing above all else: "the necessity for allowing administration to perform its discretionary functions within the area of legislative policy free from the restraining hand of the judiciary." While this had always been the Harvard approach, during the New Deal it took on the appearance of something more than a scholarly proposition. It became a fighting stance, for by the middle of the 1930s, the New Dealers believed that administrative government was being threatened by "judicial usurpation"—and, indeed, that already in many instances, "the courts rather

Press, 1970), 181–82, 208, 224–25; James A. Gross, *The Making of the National Labor Relations Board* (Albany: State University of New York Press, 1974), 52–55, 76ff., 88, 166.

17. Jaffe, "Landis," 319.

18. Quoted in Gerald Garvey, "Edward S. Corwin in the Campaign of History: The Struggle for National Power in the 1930's," *George Washington Law Review*, 34 (1965): 227.

19. Landis, "Crucial Issues," 1078.

20. Landis, *Administrative Process*, 51, 55, 67–68, 70, 75–76; Jaffe, "Landis," 319–22; William O. Douglas, *Democracy and Finance*, ed. James Allen (New Haven: Yale University Press, 1940), 243–67; Walter Gellhorn, *Fed-*

than the administrators have become the final arbiters as to the content and meaning of national legislative standards."[21]

In fact, the judges of the reviewing courts were exerting no tighter or more substantive rein on administrative decision-making than they had in the first two decades of the twentieth century. But their requirements for lawful administration had evolved in response to a more limited version of administrative government than the New Deal's, and these requirements failed to pass the New Dealer's test of the "desirability of supporting government power as a general proposition."[22] For young lawyers coming down from the mountain peaks of Frankfurter's seminar and writings and taking a close look at the case law for the first time, it seemed that the judges were crafting "technical distinctions . . . to justify their departures from the basic principle of administrative finality."[23]

Moreover, at the bar and in the Congress, there had begun to be persistent calls for the creation of an administrative court to review intensively the decisions of administrative agencies, or in some versions, to take over the agencies' power to adjudicate the controversies arising from their work. In 1933, the American Bar Association created a Special Committee on Administrative Law, and for the next half-dozen years the Committee turned out a variety of proposals to establish, in the words of one New Dealer, "a system of administrative justice based solely on the nebulous concept of a judicial or quasi-judicial function."[24] At the same time, Senator Marvel M. Logan, a Kentucky Democrat, was introducing an administrative court bill in almost every session of Congress. His 1939 offering adopted the current proposals of the ABA's Special Com-

---

eral Administrative Proceedings (Baltimore: Johns Hopkins Press, 1941), 43; Jerome Frank, *If Men Were Angels* (New York: Harper, 1942), 181.

21. Robert M. Cooper, "Administrative Justice and the Role of Discretion," *Yale Law Journal*, 47 (1938): 596–97.

22. Garvey, "Corwin," 227.

23. Cooper, "Administrative Justice," 596.

24. Robert M. Cooper, "The Proposed United States Administrative Court," *Michigan Law Review*, 35 (1937): 566–67.

mittee and passed the Congress, only to fall before a presidential veto.[25]

For the scholarly lawyers of the New Deal, these events seemed to make clear the urgent necessity of demonstrating to the legal profession and to the Congress the correctness of respecting the finality of administrative decisions. In articles and lectures, in the reports of governmental and privately sponsored investigations of administrative law and practice, and in judicial opinions—Frankfurter and William O. Douglas were elevated to the Supreme Court in 1939—the New Deal lawyers presented their view of the matter.

Formerly, in the era when Wyman wrote, the relation of the judicial function to the substantive problems of administrative government had appeared to be a complex legal question. Wyman had struggled long and hard to make a plausible demonstration of his scheme for keeping the courts at arm's length from administration. And in doing this, he was not moved by the "desirability of supporting government power as a general proposition,"[26] but by considerations having to do with the place of public law in the Harvard model of legal education. But for the New Dealers, the issue was much less complex and essentially nonlegal.

It seemed obvious that a regime of expertise was suited to the tasks of administrative government and that a judicial approach was not. Therefore what the proponents of judicial involvement were really talking about was leaving the tasks of modern government undone. It might be claimed that a judicial approach would promote the justice and efficiency of the administrative process, but the New Deal lawyers knew that these were mere "slogans" and that "the material interests whose nakedness they cover" were the real story. A hankering

25. Maxwell S. Isenburgh, "Developments in Administrative Law, 1930–1940," *Virginia Law Review*, 27 (1940): 29–74; Report of the Special Committee on Administrative Law, American Bar Association, *Reports*, 58 (1933): 407–27; Louis L. Jaffe, "Invective and Investigation in Administrative Law," *Harvard Law Review*, 52 (1939): 1221–42.

26. Garvey, "Corwin," 227.

after the lost world of *laissez faire* in economics, law, and government, and an insufficient commitment to the cause of social justice, were the motives.[27]

The issue of judicial involvement—and ultimately of a substantive administrative law—was political, not legal, for the New Deal lawyers, and they believed that they had considerable evidence for their view. The analyses of administrative government by the ABA's Special Committee on Administrative Law, for instance, were superficial and hastily composed, and it was obvious that at the bar many of the advocates of an administrative court were not the staunchest friends of the New Deal. These lawyers did little to conceal their hope that a transfer to a court of the questions adjudicated by an agency like the National Labor Relations Board might result in different substantive results. On the bench, the Supreme Court's striking down of New Deal legislation seemed to speak for itself. And in Congress, it hardly seemed a coincidence that one of Senator Logan's bills finally won passage at a time when a coalition of Republicans and conservative Democrats attained the zenith of its influence during the New Deal.[28]

While the New Deal lawyers were not mistaken about the politics of much of the support for a greater judicial involvement in administrative government, what is striking about their attitude is that they saw the issue almost *solely* as a political ploy. As a serious intellectual issue in law, it was nonexistent for them. The completeness of Harvard's victory in legal education and scholarship, now four decades old, the crisis of the Depression with its need for immediate governmental action and the need to believe in the efficacy of that action, and the New Dealers' own youthfulness, obscured the

27. Jaffe, "Invective and Investigation," 1245 (quotations); Landis, "Crucial Issues," 1078.

28. Jaffe, "Invective and Investigation," 1222–36; Landis, "Crucial Issues," 1078; George Wolfskill, *The Revolt of the Conservatives* (Boston: Houghton Mifflin, 1962), 70–78; Jacob M. Lashly, "Administrative Law and the Bar," *Virginia Law Review*, 25 (1939): 641–58; James T. Patterson, *Congressional Conservatism and the New Deal* (Lexington: University of Kentucky Press, 1967), 288–324.

fact that a substantive judicial involvement with the administrative process had once been regarded as a legal issue of great significance. Thus, when Chief Justice Charles Evans Hughes suggested in 1938 that administrative agencies, "which we earnestly desire to succeed . . . , will achieve that end to the extent that they perform their work with the recognized responsibility which attaches to judges,"[29] the only sense that a young lawyer like Walter Gellhorn could make of such a statement was that Hughes no doubt "throughout his career . . . manifested a distrust of the administrative process."[30] Likewise, Gellhorn simply could not imagine that anything but political enlightenment moved someone like Justice Stone to be "tolerant and understanding" of the administrative process.[31]

Yet, though they were expressions of dislike for the politics of the New Deal, the proposals of the ABA's Special Committee and the passage of the Logan Bill by Congress were also expressions of the kind of second thoughts that Chief Justice Hughes was having about the nature of the administrative process. As governor of New York in 1907, Hughes had done more than any one individual in the twentieth century to launch modern administrative government. For thirty years he had been one of its defenders, and he continued to be. But observing the administrative fever of the New Deal lawyers, Hughes had begun to wonder whether "the desire to emphasize the importance of obtaining flexibility in particular classes of cases, [and] to depreciate the work of courts and by comparison to exalt administrative boards and commissions" was not "shortsighted and . . . not in the interest of the suitable development of administrative agencies."[32]

29. Charles Evans Hughes, "Address of the Chief Justice," American Law Institute, *Proceedings*, 15 (1938): 37.

30. Walter Gellhorn, "Stone on Administrative Law," *Columbia Law Review*, 46 (1946): 735.

31. Ibid.; and see pp. 122–23, above.

32. Hughes, "Address," 36–37 (quotations); as for Hughes' administrative pedigree, see pp. 76–77, 84, above, and Charles Evans Hughes, "Some Aspects of the Development of American Law," New York State Bar Associa-

By the 1930s, however, there was little possibility for the development of this perspective, for the best legal minds would have nothing to do with it. When, for example, the ABA's Special Committee on Administrative Law solicited Felix Frankfurter's advice on an administrative court bill, it was met with a caution against "premature generalizations. . . . I should much rather have the committee restrict itself for the present to luminous examination of the actual operations of our administrative tribunals before proposing legislative measures in regard to them."[33] When the Committee went ahead anyway, the defects of its proposals were easily exposed by Frankfurter's protégés, while the implications of an administrative court system were ignored by them. The scholarly lawyers of the New Deal were willing to support the development of administrative law along procedural lines only. As for the substance of administrative decisions, there they knew that expertise reigned and justified the rule of finality.[34]

By means of an opinion-making power that their opponents could not match, these New Dealers "won" their battle in the late 1930s and early 1940s. The attention of the legal profession and the Congress was directed away from a brief and mainly politically inspired flirtation with administrative courts and back to a concern with the procedural context of administrative decision-making.

---

tion, *Reports*, 39 (1916): 269–70; opinion of Hughes, Morgan v. United States, 298 U.S. 468 (1936), at pp. 480–81; as for second thoughts, see Ferrel Heady and Eleanor Tabor Linenthal, "Congress and Administrative Regulation," *Law and Contemporary Problems*, 26 (1961): 238–45; James O. Freedman, "Crisis and Legitimacy in the Administrative Process," *Stanford Law Review*, 27 (1975): 1044, 1051–56; remarks of O. R. McGuire, "Report of the Cincinnati Conference on Functions and Procedure of Administrative Tribunals," *University of Cincinnati Law Review*, 12 (1938): 158–60; Lashly, "Administrative Law," 641–58.

33. Felix Frankfurter to Louis G. Caldwell, May 11, 1934, Frankfurter MSS, box 188, folder 2, Harvard Law School Library (quotation); also see Caldwell to Frankfurter, May 1, 1934, ibid.

34. John Dickinson, "The Acheson Report: A Novel Approach to Administrative Law," *University of Pennsylvania Law Review*, 90 (1942): 757–59, 770–75; remarks of John Dickinson, in *The Federal Administrative Procedure Act and the Administrative Agencies*, ed. George Warren (New York:

This, of course, had always been the basic orientation of the American legal system, and it was one that had been solidified by the 1930s in case law and, at the bar, in habits of practice of many years' standing. But for the young scholars who believed themselves to be living through the "formative years" of their subject, it seemed that a fundamental choice of direction had presented itself, with the future of politically enlightened and expert government hanging in the balance. By the mid-1940s, they felt that they had been through a tough fight and had achieved a great victory, for in administrative government the law seemed to revolve like a satellite around a sun of expertise.[35]

3

And then, very quickly, it was gone. From the perspective of the early 1950s, it seemed to a New Deal veteran like Louis Jaffe that only yesterday, "The administrative process was thought to have an inherent political or social orientation. There was more or less agreement as to its significance between those who hailed it and those who hated it. It was seen with hope by the one and fear by the other as capable of working continually progressive modification of the economy and society. Supplanting private industry, it would take over the role of leadership in the 'public interest.' This was not, we can see now, a just historical estimate."[36]

Coming out of the sunlight of the New Deal, a clear look at

New York University School of Law, 1947), 548–61, 578–79; Louis G. Caldwell, "Federal Communications Commission—Comments on the Report of the Staff of the Attorney General's Committee," *George Washington Law Review*, 8 (1940): 750–52, 816–18; A. H. Feller, "Administrative Law Investigation Comes of Age," *Columbia Law Review*, 41 (1941): 589–616.

35. *Final Report of the Attorney General's Committee on Administrative Procedure* (Washington: Government Printing Office, 1941); Warren, ed., *Administrative Procedure Act*; Schwartz, *Administrative Law*, 19–21.

36. Louis L. Jaffe, "The Effective Limits of the Administrative Process," *Harvard Law Review*, 67 (1954): 1105 (quotation); also see Ritchie, *Landis*, 155; Bernard Schwartz, "The Administrative World of Mr. Justice Frankfurter," *Yale Law Journal*, 59 (1950): 1265.

the performance of administrators exploded the notion of a regime of expertise. Lawyers and legal scholars now saw what had always been there to see:

> . . . agency opinions contain almost no clear statements of general principle. They are almost always enormously long and filled with facts and statistics, but the reader usually looks in vain for a statement of the basic principles on which the case was decided and on which similar cases presumably will be decided in the future. . . . Since they never seem to come to grips with the real problems and policy issues involved in . . . regulatory activities, they are of little interest.[37]

Such decisions were only cosmetic. If there were occasional decisions that meant something, the real disposition of administrative power more often took place during informal proceedings whose fairness and fundamental lawfulness could not be determined in the record of the formal proceedings capable of being reviewed by appellate court judges. Off the record, administrators usually operated not according to calculations of the "public interest," but according to calculations of their self-interest, accommodating the predominant pressures of the moment.[38]

Such behavior, of course, had been remarked upon as early as the Progressive Era. But then it had been assumed that expertise was merely going through the rough early stages of its development, that its maturity would bring different results. Later, needing to believe in the efficacy of governmental action in the face of a terrifying depression, many Americans during the New Deal convinced themselves that this stage had been reached. And thus, in the late 1940s and early 1950s, they found it difficult to excuse nonexpert administrative performance on account of youth—indeed, some observers began to wonder if the administrative process had not hit old age.[39]

37. Louis J. Hector, "Government by Anonymity: Who Writes Our Regulatory Opinions?" *American Bar Association Journal*, 45 (1959): 1260.

38. Bernard Schwartz, *The Professor and the Commissions* (New York: Knopf, 1959), 115ff.

39. Jaffe, "Effective Limits," 1109.

This crash of expectations was paralleled by developments in public administration theory. The "science" of public administration had coalesced by the beginning of the 1930s, lending intellectual substance to the New Deal's hopes for the administrative process, but also exposing its assumptions to revisionists in the 1940s and 1950s. Critics demonstrated "how value-loaded, how culture-bound, how political—in short, how 'unscientific'—were the premises, the 'principles,' the logic, of orthodox public administration."[40]

For legal scholars who "had looked to the administrative process with such exalted expectations," the performance of the post–New Deal agencies was "a particularly bitter experience."[41] In a post-expertise administrative world, the New Deal veterans had to agree with Harvard's Louis Jaffe that it was now necessary to "face facts": the administrative process had always been "basically an experiment" into which Americans out of overly exuberant but good intentions had read unrealistic potentials.[42]

According to Jaffe, Americans had in essence transferred some of the unsolved problems of the legislative process to the administrative process, as if a different name could produce different results. And while the unique circumstances of the New Deal had obscured this reality, it was now possible to see that "a political conflict [cannot] be avoided by relegating a problem to the care of an agency and invoking the talisman of 'expertise.' The effect of such a transfer of function is simply to shift the legislative process to a different level, and there is no reason to believe that the agency will be able to rise above the power conflicts to achieve solutions that the legislature itself cannot or does not choose to provide."[43]

This is not to say that the administrative agency does not continue "to be a valuable tool of government." After all, those

40. Wallace S. Sayre, "Premises of Public Administration: Past and Emerging," *Public Administration Review*, 18 (1958): 104.

41. Jaffe, "Landis," 324.

42. Jaffe, "Illusion," 1184, 1197; the arguments of this article were anticipated in Jaffe's "Effective Limits" article of 1954 (note 36, above).

43. Jaffe. "Illusion," 1190.

who had believed so fervently in the administrative process during the New Deal could not have been entirely mistaken about it. "There are many day-to-day tasks that cannot be otherwise performed. Give an agency a decently defined mandate, adequate funds, its due quota of 'men of average capabilities' and it will do a good job."[44] But "the key to success is the strong and persistent public opinion which demands a response to a given problem, which is sufficiently organized to press for the detailed legislative solution required, and which will, ultimately, keep the administration on the job of implementing it."[45]

Without this legislative solution, the substance of an administrative decision, which once was thought to be the domain of experts seeking objective criteria for the "public interest," ought now to be seen as basically a political debate among citizens interested in the result. Some students of administrative government may, of course, continue to believe that the administrator can find some nonpolitical technique to supply answers to problems which the legislature could not resolve and therefore passed along to him. But this will only result in "false implications" and "ill-founded and futile criticisms." The truth of the matter is that, "if, given the conflict of political forces, the agency gets no further than Congress itself was able to get, there is very little basis for criticism"[46]—not of the agency, not very much of Congress even, and certainly not of those who once believed in a regime of expertise.

4

In Jaffe's analysis, one's understanding of the nature of administrative decision-making was to change, but nothing else. He was interested only in explaining what had gone wrong with the great hope of his youth. The political contest at the heart of the administrative process was to be played out with the same procedural rules of administrative law that Jaffe had

44. Jaffe, "Landis," 324.
45. Jaffe, "Illusion," 1198.
46. Ibid., 1194, 1198.

learned in his youth—with rules, that is, evolved for what was then presumed to be a rational and progressive search by experts for the "public interest." But scholars younger than Jaffe were not satisfied with this state of affairs. A different game seemed to need different rules.[47]

By this point in the century, of course, the old fears of legal scholarship regarding administrative government had been moot for decades and were quite beyond the consciousness of contemporary scholars.[48] Indeed, on the surface in legal education, the world of Ames and Beale that had called forth those fears seemingly had vanished into the mists of time. Except for the first year, the concerns of the curriculum appeared utterly transformed, with scores of electives on almost every legal and quasi-legal subject imaginable.[49]

Yet beneath this surface appearance, the parsing of the cases of the regular courts remained the core of the experience in all but a few courses, and special skill at case-parsing remained the only way of advancement into the ranks of legal scholarship. Legal education remained as unconcerned as it had been in Freund's day with searching for the true dimensions of the modern legal order—as opposed to letting students drift from one case-parsing experience to another. And most important, perhaps, what might be called the "Powell syndrome" continued unabated; that is, the delusion of legal scholars that from the routine of their law school lives they know what they are about in law. According to one scholar of the late 1960s, his fraternity possessed,

47. Ibid., 1197; G. Edward White, "Allocating Power Between Agencies and Courts: The Legacy of Justice Brandeis," *Duke Law Journal* (1974): 240; Nathaniel L. Nathanson, "The Contributions of Louis L. Jaffe to Administrative Law," *Harvard Law Review*, 89 (1976): 1667–79; Philippe Nonet, *Administrative Justice* (New York: Russell Sage Foundation, 1969), 5; Richard B. Stewart, "The Reformation of American Administrative Law," *Harvard Law Review*, 88 (1975): 1669–70; Bernard Schwartz, *Administrative Law* (Boston: Little, Brown, 1976), 16–24.

48. See pp. 39–40, 67–68, 92–93, 143, above.

49. Joel Seligman, *The High Citadel* (Boston: Houghton Mifflin, 1978). 66–67, 81; Archibald Cox, review of Joel Seligman, *The High Citadel* (1978), in *Harvard Law Review*, 92 (1979): 1172.

a special capacity for dispassionate analysis, a clear-eyed regard for the facts, an open-minded willingness to look at a problem from every side, a human historical perspective that enables us to perceive problems in their full context, a nose for detecting trouble in advance, and a talent as conceptual architects to design imaginative adaptations to head it off.[50]

50. Bayless Manning, "Introduction: New Tasks for Lawyers," in Geoffrey C. Hazard, ed., *Law in a Changing America* (Englewood Cliffs, N.J.: Prentice Hall, 1968), 11; Manning was the dean of the Stanford Law School at this time, and I assume that what he considered to be the qualities of lawyers in general he would have attributed to the elite of lawyers, the law professors and legal scholars. For the Powell syndrome, see chap. 4, sec. 2, above. For the changelessness of the core of legal education, see Seligman, *High Citadel*, 10, 71, 127, 131, 145, 149–59, 182–85.

A more recent example of the Powell syndrome is Archibald Cox's 1979 review of Seligman's book, which is a critical account of the modern-day Harvard Law School. First Cox tells his readers that: "The lawyer is a free society's principal expert in working out those mechanisms, accommodations and constraints [necessary to social order]. He specializes in creating and operating the procedures into which we channel conflicts. . . . [He] is engaged in helping people live together in the pursuit and achievement of individual goals with a minimum of force and a maximum of reason—helping them live in ways that soften and often substitute for power and thus offer man's best hope of liberty, of mutual respect for human dignity, and of . . . progress" (p. 1170). Then Cox asks, "Why are lawyers [so] creative?" Well, it seems that: "A major source of the lawyer's creativity is the peculiar mix of human understanding and intellectual discipline that fills the lawyer's life. The law's concerns are men and women, their daily lives, their fears and aspirations, their mean pursuits and high adventures. The true lawyer will know and understand them better than they know themselves. . . . With these instruments the lawyer also acquires the sense of relevance that separates the essential from the trivial and the primary from the subordinate" (p. 1178). And where, in the first instance, does the lawyer acquire these vast powers? Why, from the case method in law school, of course: "The essence of the case method—the problem method or discussion method, if you prefer—is the *critical* examination of a problem from every angle as one strips away the leaves in the search for the heart. . . . Given this degree of flexibility, the case or problem method seems to me to stimulate forms of creative thought paralleling the chief form of progress in human institutions" (p. 1180). Almost as an afterthought Cox does concede that: "*The High Citadel* is essentially accurate, however, in taxing all of us with the proposition that no major law school has ever studied or is studying the overall performance of the legal profession, including the courts. . . . A fortiori no student leaves his law school with an overall view of the profession, of its accomplishments

Thus, it was not surprising that, perceiving something to be amiss with administrative government, the "cleverest men"[51] in law in the late 1960s set out to create a new administrative law for a post-expertise world.

A first step in its creation was to arrive at an explanation more plausible than Jaffe's for why the old administrative law had come to be built around expertise. Good intentions and overexuberance seemed rather tenuous in a time frame of almost eighty years. Granted, the New Deal was a special case, but would not Americans and especially lawyers have realized during the preceding half century that they were dealing with an essentially political process?

The answer to this puzzle was provided in 1966 by Charles A. Reich of the Yale Law School.[52] Reich suggested that while the nature of administrative decision-making had been essentially political for most of the twentieth century, this was not necessarily the case at the turn of the century. "When the

---

and omissions, or of the benefits conferred upon society measured against the costs. He does not even get this view of the operation of the judicial system" (p. 1182). But, then, when one "thinks like a lawyer," who cares? Or as Cox puts it more gently (and here we see shades of Ames, Gray, Beale, Frankfurter, and even the failed "law and society" experimenters of the 1920s): "What justifies such seemingly grave omissions? Is it vapid to think of a broad study of the sociological impact of the legal profession because the subject is too large? Can the broad question be broken down into more manageable parts without losing unity? Can the sociological impact and omissions of courts and lawyers be studied apart from review of substantive law? Although I have no answers to these questions, I sense that the studies will be made, if not by the legal profession then by outsiders. Where better to undertake the work than in the law schools? Law professors alone would be incompetent, but at a university they can team with experts from other disciplines. . . . There can be few better subjects for a large foundation's grant than a feasibility study of this area, looking optimistically to a longer and vaster undertaking. Along the way teaching materials for a series of required courses might develop" (p. 1182). But that is really neither here nor there. After all, as Thomas Reed Powell understood, anyone who knows the American people better than they know themselves also knows that he is doing it right already. See Cox, review of *The High Citadel*, at the pages noted.

51. James Barr Ames, "Christopher Columbus Langdell." *Lectures in Legal History* (Cambridge: Harvard University Press, 1913), 480.

52. Also of *The Greening of America* (New York: Random House, 1970).

federal government first undertook regulation in a major way, in the case of the railroads, Congress created the Interstate Commerce Commission to deal with this specific problem. . . . The job of the ICC was to *regulate*, that is, to police activities which otherwise remained essentially private."[53] At the turn of the century, then, "it is possible that 'the public interest' had a different, more definite meaning than it does now. In times dominated by economic pillage, robber barons, and piratical business tactics, 'the public interest' could simply mean not yielding to private interest; perhaps it was reasonably clear what was *not* in the public interest. That may have been enough for early forms of regulation."[54]

Reich, apparently, was unaware that during the Progressive Era state commissions like New York's possessed broader powers than did the ICC. He believed that it was not until after the First World War that burdens were placed on American administrative government that were substantially different from policing robber barons. Only then could he find an agency like the Federal Communications Commission which,

> although described as if it were merely regulating traffic on the airways, engages not only in regulation but also in *allocation*; it licenses private companies to use the scarce and valuable channels of the radio spectrum. Likewise the Civil Aeronautics Board allocates routes for air transportation and the Federal Power Commission allocates natural gas pipeline routes and hydroelectric sites. Still further from the original function is the growing responsibility of some agencies to engage in *planning*.[55]

For such tasks, there is no objective "public interest" standard. Decisions as to "what kind of television programs Boston should have, or which city should get a regional airport" involve "almost purely a value choice" of a kind traditionally made in legislatures and not elsewhere.[56]

53. Charles A. Reich, "The Law of the Planned Society," *Yale Law Journal*, 75 (1966): 1231.

54. Ibid., 1234.

55. Ibid., 1231.

56. Ibid., 1236.

Thus, according to Reich, the nature of administrative decision-making was not always "essentially political," but it certainly was by the 1960s. And this explained what had happened to the old administrative law. It had been a response to the needs of a turn-of-the-century administrative government whose simple tasks could be accomplished with a technique like expertise. As the twentieth century advanced, this administrative law proved increasingly inadequate, but the cause really lay with administrative government and, ultimately, with American society.

As America grew both more interdependent and more pluralistic, the legislature had increasingly attempted to rationalize the people's tangled affairs, and almost always by passing them along to the administrative process. By mid-century, administrators were little more than moderators of a national town meeting—as one scholar put it, "[p]rivate ordering has been swallowed up by government, while government has become in part a species of private ordering."[57] Under such circumstances, Reich believed, an administrative law built around expertise could do little except "preserve the mythology about how government operates."[58]

What, then, was to be done? Jaffe had suggested that administrators could operate in an essentially political environment if there was public agreement on the proper response to a given problem. But in late twentieth-century America, this appeared a vain hope. The spirit of the age seemed all opposed to it, and many Americans had taken for their governmental philosophy something like a "barebones liberalism which is . . . committed only to the belief that tolerance is a primary virtue and that a diversity of opinions and habits is not only to be endured but to be cherished and encouraged."[59]

Yet some legal scholars, as well as some practitioners and

57. Stewart, "Reformation of Administrative Law," 1760.

58. Reich, "Law of the Planned Society," 1237.

59. Judith N. Shklar, *Legalism* (Cambridge: Harvard University Press, 1964), 5 (quotation); also see Bernard Schwartz and H. W. R. Wade, *Legal Control of Government* (Oxford: Clarendon Press, 1972), 7; G. Edward White, "The Evolution of Reasoned Elaboration: Jurisprudential Criticism

judges, believed that they had an answer. An administrative process which under the mantle of expertise had become an exercise in inertia could be made over into "a structure of opportunities for participation and criticism, allowing affected persons to challenge and influence official policy."[60] Administrators would be required by administrative law to heed (or perhaps "cherish") a greater diversity of opinions in the course of their deliberations. Particularly this was an attractive course to those lawyers who called themselves, ironically in a post-expertise age, "public interest lawyers":

> Public interest lawyers believe that the system as it now exists can be used very effectively, provided proper legal initiatives are taken to utilize the procedures of the agencies to initiate cases in the public interest. . . . The feeling is that if one knows the rules of the game and is able to manipulate them, the legal processes of the agencies can be used to advantage.
>
> Recognizing that the outputs of administrative agencies are determined primarily on the basis of constituency inputs, citizen groups are increasingly becoming active administrative constituents.[61]

Indeed, by the mid-1970s, there had been such rapid progress in administrative practice, in legal thinking, and in the case law of the reviewing courts, that Professor Richard B. Stewart of the Harvard Law School was able to attempt a preliminary synthesis of recent developments.[62]

Administrative decision-making, Stewart found, was now conceived of as an occasion for political debate by citizens interested in its results, and the primary function of administrative law was becoming "the provision of a surrogate political process to ensure the fair representation of a wide range of affected interests."[63] Under this diagnosis, the problem of ad-

---

and Social Change," *Virginia Law Review*, 59 (1973): 296; Stewart, "Reformation of Administrative Law," 1770–81.

60. Nonet, *Administrative Justice*, 6 (italics omitted).

61. Peter Woll, "Administrative Law in the Seventies," *Public Administration Review*, 32 (1972): 561.

62. Stewart, "Reformation of Administrative Law," 1669–71, 1711ff.; also see Schwartz, *Administrative Law*, 22–24.

63. Stewart, "Reformation of Administrative Law," 1670.

ministrative procedure was "to provide representation for all affected interests; the problem of substantive policy . . . to reach equitable accommodations among these interests . . . ; and the problem of judicial review . . . to ensure that agencies provide fair procedures for representation and reach fair accommodations."[64]

Like other observers in the 1970s, Stewart found this development preferable to that of the preceding decades when administrative law had been built wholly around expertise. But he also found a disturbing prospect in this new administrative law. Implicit in its development was "the assumption that there is no ascertainable, transcendent 'public interest,' but only the distinct interests of various individuals and groups in society";[65] and in a society as diverse and complex as that of late twentieth-century America, the distinct interests affected by any given administrative action could be almost limitless, or least beyond the limits of manageable government.[66]

If the present trend continued, the hearing and decisional processes of agencies would become crowded beyond capacity with the claims and counterclaims of a quarrelsome citizenry. What had seemed to be a hopeful course now seemed to portend turmoil. But given the political nature of administrative decision-making, there seemed to be no alternative except to continue to treat the administrative process as "a surrogate political process"[67] for a multitude of vexatious interests. There was no way, apparently, for administrators to articulate, even for a portion of the controversies committed to them, a shared sense of what was good order, or of what kind of society their decisions were to advance. There was, in short, "no . . . 'public interest,' but only the distinct interests."[68] And thus it

64. Ibid., 1759; presumably, the test of a fair accommodation would be whether the agency gave the evidence presented by each interest the weight due it.

65. Ibid., 1712.

66. Ibid., 1770–1813; also see Philippe Nonet and Philip Selznick, *Law and Society in Transition* (New York: Octagon Books, 1978), 102–3.

67. Stewart, "Reformation of Administrative Law," 1670.

68. Ibid., 1712.

almost seemed as if legal scholarship should now impose upon the administrative process the image of an unknit society, the very disorder of which was originally the reason for calling that process forth.

That wasn't going to happen, of course. Those men who prided themselves above all else on their power to think and to solve problems wouldn't let it happen, or at least not completely.

Throughout the late 1970s and into the 1980s, therefore, legal scholars continued to bring forth their ruminations for making a go of administrative government. But held in the grip of historical and institutional forces that they could not begin to comprehend, they seemed incapable of seeking out long-term solutions. Rather, it appeared increasingly likely that the contribution of legal scholarship would continue to be mere interstitial law-jobbing against a backdrop of an almost total misapprehension of how the present state of administrative affairs came to be.[69]

As for the future of administrative law and government, we might observe along with one legal scholar that we "seem to be moving toward a new period whose essential outlines are not yet clear."[70]

69. For example, Paul R. Verkuil, "The Emerging Concept of Administrative Procedure," *Columbia Law Review*, 78 (1978): 261–79; however, an interesting, if partial, exception is Robert L. Rabin, "Administrative Law in Transition: A Discipline in Search of an Organizing Principle," *Northwestern University Law Review*, 72 (1977): 120–45. In somewhat larger context, the intellectual confusion of American public law scholarship is suggested by Mark Tushnet, "Truth, Justice, and the American Way: An Interpretation of Public Law Scholarship in the Seventies," *Texas Law Review*, 57 (1979): 1316–45; and the degree to which American lawyers are culture-bound in their assumptions about the nature of law—a result at least in part of the disinterest of law teachers and scholars in trying to see the law whole—is suggested by Linda Medcalf, *Law and Identity* (Beverly Hills, Calif.: Sage Publications, 1978), esp. pp. 17–20, 27–30, 108–12.

70. Schwartz, *Administrative Law*, 22.

Postscript and Prospect

In attempting to chart a course for the future, the legal scholars of the present would do well to look to the past—both their own and that of administrative government. That is not to say that the past visited upon the present would remake the world. The imposing edifice of present-day administrative government will not crash into dust. In the hundred years since its appearance, powerful clienteles—in Congress, at the bar, and among the regulated—have grown up around the administrative process, calcifying its initially random and haphazard form. The present situation by and large simply must be lived with—and often with good results, let us be clear. Expertise—not the expertise of Progressive Era fancy, but a decent, middling expertise—is alive and well here and there in the process. Nevertheless, the discovery of an administrative (and an administrative law) past different from the one commonly imagined ought to alter substantially the morale and psychology of those who propose the incremental adjustments to administrative government that occasionally seem feasible.

For if anything seems clear from the historical record as it has been portrayed here, it is that the administrative process did not evolve on its own terms, that the channel it ultimately dug for itself was not wholly a product of pragmatic testing against the realities, obsessions, complexities, and myths of American life—although that is the common impression, thanks to the labors of Felix Frankfurter, especially. The administrative process, in other words, is not necessarily a reflection of the America that was and is; the limitations of the process are not necessarily the imprints of the points at which the other processes of American life would not give, could not overcome their natures to achieve a different result in administration.

In particular, it would be a mistake to depreciate, on the basis of what has been wrought in administration, the capacity of American politics to work toward satisfying results in government. The ultimate shape of the administrative process was hardly *mandated* by the infatuation of early twentieth-century politics with the concept of expertise, for instance. Administrative experiments that cut in a different direction, a judicial direction, were spurned by the public and its representatives in one very important sense simply because no intellectual justification for such experiments existed. Existed, that is, before the public.

Yet, ironically, disenchanted though we have become with the administrative process and with the political process that at least formally created it, today we have turned increasingly to a reliance upon the judicial function in the shape of the federal courts, and one, moreover, that is uninformed by what could have been almost a century's experience with judicial policy-making in administration. The public policy function of the judge, had it been permitted by legal scholarship to evolve in due course in the justiciable areas of the administrative process and thus to strengthen that process, might also have strengthened our regard for elective politics as the creator of the process. But because an understanding of the judicial function in administration was suppressed and the process faltered, we now depreciate elective politics and give perhaps too much of our governmental destiny over to the life appointees of the federal judiciary, who are relative babes in the woods when it comes to understanding the public policy implications of their offices. Present-day administration might be difficult of adjustment, but from the historical record of its evolution, we might at least wish to think better of ourselves as a political people and of our capacity for creative self-government.

Of course, when it comes down to precise proposals for governmental change, that "we" of the preceding paragraph often becomes only a small part of us: legal scholars. They will have the final word as to what, if anything, the past says to the present. And they would do well in this regard, as has been said, to heed their own past as well as that of administration.

For what has been called the "Powell syndrome" continues unabated to the present day, and within the university, today as yesterday, the law school is simply another world. And yet, undoubtedly, it is from that world that the suggestions for the future course of the American republic in its administrative and judicial aspects will finally come.

Note on Sources / Index

A Note on Sources, Challenges, and Boundaries in Legal and Administrative History

Because so much of this study is based upon law review literature, much of it highly specialized, a complete bibliography would be needlessly long. Using the *Index to Legal Periodicals* and its predecessors, the researcher can readily make a complete search of a major portion of the intellectual output of legal scholars; for, with the exception of an occasional treatise, they rarely write books. All that I attempt to do here, then, is mention some of my concerns in relation to the literature of this study, some of the works that provide an opening upon that literature, and a few titles that either were particularly valuable for me or might otherwise go unnoticed.

Manuscripts

Collections not cited in the notes which provided valuable information are the papers of Henry M. Hart, Calvert Magruder, and Charles E. Wyzanski, Manuscript Division, Harvard Law School Library; the papers of Joel Parker and Emory Washburn, Massachusetts Historical Society; and the Thomas Mott Osborne Papers, The George Arents Research Library, Syracuse University.

Reports and Proceedings of Private Associations

The *Reports* of the American Bar Association are a valuable resource, particularly for the years 1892 to 1946. The annual reports of the following committees and sections of the Association are of particular interest: Section of Legal Education, for the years 1893 to 1920; Section of Public Utility Law, 1918–34; Special Committee on Administrative Law, 1933–46; Standing Committee on Air Law, 1927–28, followed by the Committee on Radio Law, 1929, and the Committee on Communications, 1930.

The reports of state bar associations can provide something of the same service for their geographical areas and level of regulatory concern—in this case, the *Reports* of the New York State Bar Association, consulted for the years 1905 to 1920. Additionally, the *Proceedings* of the National Association of Railway [and public utility] Commissioners are of some value for clarifying the concerns and problems of governmental regulation, especially during the Progressive Era.

Legal Education and Scholarship

There are but two general histories of American legal education that can be consulted with profit: Alfred Z. Reed, *Training for the Public Profession of the Law* (New York: Carnegie Foundation for the Advancement of Teaching, 1921), and Robert B. Stevens, "Two Cheers for 1870: The American Law School," *Perspectives in American History*, 5 (1971): 405–548. However, two useful studies with somewhat narrower focuses are William R. Johnson, *Schooled Lawyers: A Study in the Clash of Professional Cultures* (New York: New York University Press, 1978), and G. Edward White, *Tort Law in America: An Intellectual History* (New York: Oxford University Press, 1980); and one with a focus larger than just legal education and scholarship is John W. Johnson, *American Legal Culture, 1908–1940* (Westport, Conn.: Greenwood Press, 1981).

For the Harvard Law School, Arthur E. Sutherland, *The Law at Harvard: A History of Ideas and Men, 1817–1967* (Cambridge: The Belknap Press of Harvard University Press, 1967) blandly presents the basic story. This could be supplemented with Charles Warren, *History of the Harvard Law School and of Early Legal Conditions in America* (New York: Lewis Publishing Co., 1908), and most definitely should be with the *Centennial History of the Harvard Law School, 1817–1917* (Cambridge: Harvard Law School Association, 1918), whose bibliography is exhaustive for Harvard and university legal education generally in the period 1870 to 1917. Unfortunately, the manuscript sources for Harvard in the last third of the nineteenth century are very meager. To my mind, a very reliable observer of events at Harvard in this period and beyond is Samuel Williston, in *Life and Law: An Autobiography* (Boston: Little, Brown, 1940). A useful Nader study of the modern Harvard Law School is Joel Seligman, *The High Citadel: The Influence of Harvard Law School* (Boston: Houghton Mifflin, 1978). A remarkable memoir of the first-year student experience at Harvard is Scott Turow, *One L* (New York: Putnam, 1977).

For the rise of the case method generally, one would do well, again, to consult the bibliography of the *Centennial History*. The single most important reference, and the classic one, is Josef Redlich, *The Common Law and the Case Method in American University Law Schools* (New York: Carnegie Foundation for the Advancement of Teaching, 1914). Not consulted was a work in progress by William La Piana.

An important analysis of the professionalization of law teaching is Jerold S. Auerbach, "Enmity and Amity: Law Teachers and Practitioners, 1900–1922," *Perspectives in American History*, 5 (1971): 551–601. His *Unequal Justice: Lawyers and Social Change in Modern America* (New York: Oxford University Press, 1976) is of less help analytically for legal education, but it contains many useful references. Two articles from the late 1960s are particularly valuable for gauging the world view of the law teacher and scholar: Thomas F. Bergin, "The Law Teacher: A Man Divided against Himself," *Virginia Law Review*, 54 (1968): 637–57, and Lawrence M. Friedman, "Law Reform in Historical Perspective," *St. Louis University Law Journal*, 13 (1969), 351–72. Early twentieth-century estimates of the role of the law professor can be readily located through the legal indexes, the *Centennial* bibliography, the discussions of the ABA's Section on Legal Education, and the discussions and papers appearing in the *American Law School Review*. A particularly informative discussion of the place of administrative law in early twentieth-century law teaching is found in the January, 1933, issue of the *Iowa Law Review*. A discussion of value for mid-century is Bernard Schwartz, "Oversight and Oversights in Administrative Law Teaching," *Journal of Legal Education*, 11 (1959): 358–63.

The primary literature pertaining to the principal characters of this study—mostly small pieces easily identified through the periodical indexes—is large. I assume that Pound and Frankfurter are already fully accessible to historians by way of secondary sources as well. There are scarcely any secondary sources on Wyman, however, and the only reliable study of Freund is short: comment, "Ernst Freund—Pioneer of Administrative Law," *University of Chicago Law Review*, 29 (1962): 755–81. A book-length study of little interpretative help, but containing useful biographical information and a bibliography, is Oscar Kraines, *The World and Ideas of Ernst Freund: The Search for General Principles of Legislation and Administrative Law* (University, Ala.: University of Alabama Press, 1974). A useful recent biography of Landis is Donald A. Ritchie,

James M. Landis: Dean of the Regulators (Cambridge: Harvard University Press, 1980).

Administrative Law and Government

The study of administrative history is not the easiest of undertakings. In addition to the vast amount of archival material, there is the scholarship of numerous disciplines, each with its own perspectives and prescriptions, and sometimes a sense of territorial domain: law, political science, public administration, economics. This diversity of disciplines, combined with the enormity of the administrative record, produces a kaleidoscopic effect: a "reality" seen through the lens of one discipline and one administrative experience is shattered when viewed another way. But in terms of the literature, one place to start might be Thomas K. McCraw, "Regulation in America: A Review Article," *Business History Review*, 49 (1975): 159–83.

Since much of the economic literature, especially that appearing in the last two decades, concerns the question of need for regulation, I have treated it as beyond the scope of this study. However, an interesting article by a law professor that attempts to explore some of the thresholds of "unavoidable" regulation by means of both legal and economic analysis is Stephen Breyer, "Analyzing Regulatory Failure: Mismatches, Less Restrictive Alternatives, and Reform," *Harvard Law Review*, 92 (1979): 547–609. Another concern beyond the scope of this study is the intended or unintended delegation by the state of regulatory authority to private entities. There are a number of valuable works on this subject, among them, Grant McConnell, *Private Power and American Democracy* (New York: Knopf, 1966); Arthur S. Miller, *The Modern Corporate State: Private Government and the American Constitution* (Westport, Conn.: Greenwood Press, 1976); Louis L. Jaffe, "Law Making by Private Groups," *Harvard Law Review*, 51 (1937): 201–53; and Jonathan Lurie, "Commodities Exchanges as Self-Regulating Organizations in the Late 19th Century: Some Perimeters in the History of American Administrative Law," *Rutgers Law Review*, 28 (1975): 1107–40.

There is a vast literature on the nature and problems of the public administrative process, most of it from the disciplines of law and political science, and much of it dating from, or still influenced by, the era before the 1960s when regulation was often thought to be desirable *per se*. (This may be a cyclical phenomenon, in fact, and one that may return when our present "deregulation" fancy departs us.) Much of the literature is not what historians would regard as empirically based, and therefore it should be treated as merely suggesting hypotheses for research—although often very stimulating ones, I should say. Some of the authors, such as Louis Jaffe, are truly keen—indeed, brilliant—observers of the contemporary administrative process, but their observations are also exceedingly culture-bound. The nature of what lies beyond their personal experience or times—for example, the evolution of administrative law and government before the New Deal—is often dubiously formulated. (For an example of a legal scholar making this criticism of political scientists and public administrationists, see Kenneth Culp Davis, "Reflections of a Law Professor on Instruction and Research in Public Administration," *American Political Science Review*, 47 (1953): 728–52.)

There are a number of important studies of this nature that should be consulted: Louis Jaffe, "The Effective Limits of the Administrative Process: A Reevaluation," *Harvard Law Review*, 67 (1954): 1105–35, and "The Illusion of the Ideal Administration," *Harvard Law Review*, 86 (1973): 1183–99; Charles A. Reich, "The Law of the Planned Society," *Yale Law Journal*, 75 (1966): 1227–70; Richard B. Stewart, "The Reformation of American Administrative Law," *Harvard Law Review*, 88 (1975): 1699–1813; Bernard Schwartz, "The Administrative Agency in Historical Perspective," *Indiana Law Journal*, 36 (1961): 263–81; Theodore J. Lowi, *The End of Liberalism: the Second Republic of the United States*, 2nd ed. (New York: Norton, 1979), and *The Politics of Disorder* (New York: Basic Books, 1971); Henry J. Friendly (a federal appeals court judge), *The Federal Administrative Agencies: The Need for Better Definition of Standards* (Cambridge: Harvard University Press, 1962); Louis J. Hector (a practitioner and administrator), "Problems of the CAB and the Independent Regulatory Commissions," *Yale Law Journal*, 69 (1960): 931–60; Kenneth Culp Davis, *Discretionary Justice: A Preliminary Inquiry* (Baton Rouge: Louisiana State University Press, 1969); Marver H. Bernstein, "The Regulatory Process: A Framework for Analysis," *Law and Contemporary Problems*, 26 (1961): 329–46; David L. Shapiro, "The Choice of Rulemaking or Adjudication in the Development of Administrative Policy," *Harvard Law Review*, 78 (1965): 921–72; Robert L. Rabin, "Administrative Law in Transition: A Discipline in Search of an Organizing Principle," *Northwestern University Law Review*, 72 (1977): 120–45. The list could grow longer, especially from the law review literature, for which the *Index to Legal Periodicals* should be consulted. The articles of Jaffe and Schwartz are particularly useful. For the nitty-gritty of administrative law, however, the treatise work of Jaffe, Schwartz, and Davis should be consulted. Finally, a work that needs to be set apart for its special usefulness and superior historical appreciation is Philippe Nonet, *Administrative Justice: Advocacy and Change in a Government Agency* (New York: Russell Sage Foundation, 1969).

With regard to the precise historical question of how administrative law and government evolved, there is an abundance of primary material to be gathered from the law reviews (including the articles just noted)—keeping in mind, however, that whenever an author turns from a contemporary treatment of his subject to a conscious historical consideration of it, his chances of misstatement increase dramatically. Until the early 1930s, the articles are fairly infrequent, and those that have not been explicated in the text or cited in the notes can be readily located in the legal indexes. One article of importance that might escape notice, however, is Wilbur G. Katz, "Federal Legislative Courts," *Harvard Law Review*, 43 (1930): 894–924. For the New Deal years and the early 1940s, numerous observers appear, the most useful of whom I found to be Ray A. Brown, Louis G. Caldwell, A. H. Feller, Carl McFarland, Ralph F. Fuchs, J. Forrester Davison, Robert M. Cooper, Maxwell S. Isenburgh, and Fritz Morstein Marx. Many of these men continued to write, but from the late 1940s through the early 1970s, Jaffe, Schwartz, and Davis are by far the most important observers. Today, however, the field is wide open.

A legal *historian* whose work often appears in law reviews is G. Edward White, and his "Allocating Power between Agencies and Courts: The Legacy of Justice Brandeis," *Duke Law Journal*, (1974): 195–244, is particularly useful on the question of evolution. Less successful as history, but also of use, is Reginald Parker, "The Historic Basis of Administrative Law: Separation of Powers and Judicial Supremacy," *Rutgers Law Review*, 12 (1958): 449–81.

Books by legal scholars, and an occasional nonuniversity lawyer, that deal with evolution are much less numerous and usually less helpful than the articles. There are a number of "classic" studies from the 1920s through the 1940s that should be consulted, among them, Gerald C. Henderson, *The Federal Trade Commission: A Study in Administrative Law and Procedure* (New Haven: Yale University Press, 1925); Carl McFarland, *Judicial Control of the Federal*

Trade Commission and the Interstate Commerce Commission, 1920–1930 (Cambridge: Harvard University Press, 1933); Walter Gellhorn, *Federal Administrative Proceedings* (Baltimore: The Johns Hopkins Press, 1941); Joseph P. Chamberlain et al., *The Judicial Function in Federal Administrative Agencies* (New York: The Commonwealth Fund, 1942). Of the more recent literature, Bernard Schwartz, *The Professor and the Commissions* (New York: Knopf, 1959), and Martin Shapiro, *The Supreme Court and Administrative Agencies* (New York: Free Press, 1968), provide some intriguing hints. "History" of a sort also appears in the treatises. Their interpretations should be received skeptically, but they are useful to the extent of locating relevant legislative hearings, statutes, and judicial decisions.

Deserving special mention as a valuable and, for me, enigmatic observer is John Dickinson. The complexity and ambiguity of the man as suggested by his writings and the outline of his career are more than a little intriguing, but I haven't been able to gather enough satisfactory material on him to be sure, or even have solid hunches about, who he was intellectually. He appears to have been considerably more discerning than his contemporaries, but unable to make the intellectual impact on his times that he desired, due in part at least to the inhibiting power of his institutional loyalties. For the purposes of this study, his major work is *Administrative Justice and the Supremacy of Law in the United States* (Cambridge: Harvard University Press, 1927), written under the tutelage of Felix Frankfurter and Roscoe Pound (an interesting combination, since Frankfurter and Pound were bitter personal antagonists by this time). The book is nothing less than brilliant, finer than any one of Freund's works taken by itself. *Administrative Justice* is in practical effect a withering critique of the Harvard approach to administrative law and its neglect of the judicial function in the newer areas of justiciable controversy. But at the same time, Dickinson remains loyal to the very value that produced the Harvard approach: the need to preserve the traditional order in law. The best that he can suggest, therefore, is to have the regular courts assume the justiciable duties of the administrative process, clearly an impossibility by the 1920s. Dickinson's work was brilliant but stillborn. For a brief biographical sketch of Dickinson, see George L. Haskins, "John Dickinson, 1894–1952," *University of Pennsylvania Law Review*, 101 (1952): 1–25.

Turning from law to political science and public administration, there are numerous valuable titles. One might start with McCraw's review article and perhaps the writings of Marver Bernstein for political science; and for public administration, Dwight Waldo, *The Administrative State: A Study of the Political Theory of American Public Administration* (New York: Ronald Press, 1948); Frederick C. Mosher, *Democracy and the Public Service* (New York: Oxford University Press, 1968); and Wallace S. Sayre, "Premises of Public Administration: Past and Emerging," *Public Administration Review*, 18 (1958): 102–5. As a reference, Robert E. Cushman, *The Independent Regulatory Commissions* (New York: Oxford University Press, 1941), is valuable on his subject. Two particularly useful articles are John A. Fairlie, "Public Administration and Administrative Law," in Charles G. Haines and Marshall E. Dimock, eds., *Essays on the Law and Practice of Governmental Administration: A Volume in Honor of Frank Johnson Goodnow* (Baltimore: The Johns Hopkins Press, 1935); and Charles Grove Haines, "Effects of the Growth of Administrative Law upon Traditional Anglo-American Legal Theories and Practices," *American Political Science Review*, 26 (1932): 875–94. Relevant studies by historians are Barry Dean Karl, *Executive Reorganization and Reform in the New Deal: The Genesis of Administrative Management* (Cambridge: Harvard University Press, 1963); and Richard S. Kirkendall, "Franklin D. Roosevelt and the Service Intellectual," *Mississippi Valley Historical Review*, 49 (1962), 456–71. I would stress, however, the value of going directly to the primary sources in this area. The writings of political scientists and especially public administrationists convey extraordinarily well the mood of the various faiths that attached to early twentieth-century regulation.

Finally, on the question of evolution, an historical event—the creation, brief life, and death of the Commerce Court (1910–13)—provides a valuable insight into the degree to which the structure of the rising administrative process was a function of public ignorance about the nature of administrative work and the uses of the judicial function. See George E. Dix, "The Death of the Commerce Court: A Study in Institutional Weakness," *American Journal of Legal History*, 8 (1964): 238–60; George W. Rightmire, "Special Federal Courts—II: The Commerce Court," *Illinois Law Review*, 13 (1918): 97–120; Samuel O. Dunn, "The Commerce Court Question," *American Economic Review*, 3 (March 1913): 20–42; and James Wallace Bryan, "The Railroad Bill and the Court of Commerce," *American Political Science Review*, 4 (1910): 537–54.

The changing appreciation of the nature of law and the judicial function in the twentieth century—that is, the general intellectual context in which legal scholars fashioned their response to administrative government—has long been a standard concern of historians and needs no discussion here. However, two useful works may be relatively obscure: Edwin W. Patterson, *Jurisprudence: Men and Ideas of the Law* (Brooklyn: Foundation Press, 1953); and Fred V. Cahill, Jr., *Judicial Legislation: A Study in American Legal Theory* (New York: Ronald Press, 1952). And there are three useful articles in the law reviews: G. Edward White, "From Sociological Jurisprudence to Realism: Jurisprudence and Social Change in Early Twentieth-Century America," *Virginia Law Review*, 58 (1972): 999–1028, and "The Evolution of Reasoned Elaboration: Jurisprudential Criticism and Social Change," *Virginia Law Review*, 59 (1973): 279–302; and Abram Chayes, "The Role of the Judge in Public Law Litigation," *Harvard Law Review*, 89 (1976): 1281–1316.

The social cost of a legal education establishment incapable of inquiring forthrightly and analytically into the nature of a legal order of which it is a part is suggested by Linda Medcalf, *Law and Identity: Lawyers, Native Americans, and Legal Practice* (Beverly Hills, Calif.: Sage Publications, 1978).

The attitudes of the profession at large toward law, the judicial function, and the increasing powers of administrative government were also a part of the intellectual context in which legal scholars worked. These attitudes may be gleaned from the law review literature and from the reports of the ABA and the state bar associations. One particularly useful article is Cuthbert W. Pound, "The Judicial Power," *Harvard Law Review*, 35 (1922): 786–96.

One means of gauging the aspirations of legal scholars for American administrative law and practice is by looking at their attitudes toward the continental experience. The single most informative study is Bernard Schwartz, *French Administrative Law and the Common-Law World* (New York: New York University Press, 1954). Historically, of course, the story begins with Goodnow in the 1890s. About a decade later, a young political scientist, Edmund M. Parker, tried to interest legal scholars in the possibilities of the continental approach: "State and Official Liability," *Harvard Law Review*, 19 (1906): 335–49, and "Administrative Courts for the United States," American Political Science Association, *Proceedings*, 6 (1909): 46–58. From this point through the New Deal, by which time the course for administrative law and practice was set, only a handful of individuals, whose work is readily located in the legal indexes, address the question of possible lessons from the continental experience: James W. Garner, Frederick P. Walton, Stefan Riesenfeld, Edwin M. Borchard, A. H. Feller, and Fritz Morstein Marx.

Outside the world of legal scholarship proper, there have been numerous attempts over the past half century to investigate administrative government and reformulate it statutorily; the most famous being the *Final Report of the Attorney General's Committee on Administrative Procedure* (Washington: Government Printing Office, 1941), resulting (in some respects) in the Administrative Procedure Act of 1946. Since the ABA's unsuccessful venture at reformulation in 1930s, these attempts have been occasions for a flood of comment in the law reviews, a mere trickle of which, however, is of lasting value. Nevertheless, the researcher has little choice but to plow through the literature. The treatise work of Davis, Jaffe, and Schwartz provides some perspective.

Of about the same abundance, and degree of usefulness, are articles evaluating agency performance, and the fate of the researcher is the same in regard to them. But, fortunately, the literature of evaluation goes beyond the law reviews, into the realm of more readable and often more worthwhile studies by political scientists and economists (although with the latter evaluation is often an argument for deregulation). McCraw provides a useful starting point.

And it is here also that we come to contributions by historians. Most of their studies have been of individual agencies, evaluated in political or economic context, but not in legal context. I think especially of two otherwise very valuable studies, Stanley P. Caine, *The Myth of a Progressive Reform: Railroad Regulation in Wisconsin, 1903–1910* (Madison: State Historical Society of Wisconsin, 1970), and Albro Martin, *Enterprise Denied: Origins of the Decline of American Railroads, 1897–1917* (New York: Columbia University Press, 1971).

Finally, there are numerous other topics, each with its literature, that touch upon or are relevant to administrative history: arbitration, business history, bureaucracy, hearing examiners (or "administrative judges," a not very meaningful name-change of the early 1970s), judicial review, justiciability analysis, lobbying, management and policy analysis, public utility regulation (capitalization, valuation, etc.), and on and on and on. But perhaps I have said enough already to at least suggest something of the vastness and complexity of the subject. The scholar who sets sail upon its seas will not make port.

New York State

There is a wealth of material pertaining to that small part of administrative history that is the New York State Public Service Commission.

Governmental reports and publications not cited in the notes are: Public Service Commission, *Annual Report* (Albany, 1922–31); Joint Legislative Committee to Investigate the Public Service Commissions, *Minutes and Testimony*, 6 vols. (Albany: J. B. Lyon Company, 1917); *Report to the New York Legislature of the Judiciary Constitutional Convention of 1921* (Albany: J. B. Lyon Company, 1922); *Administrative Adjudication in the State of New York*, Report to the Honorable Herbert H. Lehman by Robert M. Benjamin, 6 vols. (Albany, 1942).

The archival materials of the Commission itself are contained on hundreds upon hundreds of rolls of microfilm. An opening upon this mass is provided by Charles S. Hyneman, "The Case Law of the New York Public Service Commission," *Columbia Law Review*, 34 (1934): 67–105, which sets out in fairly comprehensive fashion one view of what might be called the Commission's administrative jurisprudence as it appeared in the reports of decision from 1907 onwards. The article needs to be used with caution, however. At the time of Hyneman's study, the by now consolidated Commission was headed by Milo Maltbie, an FDR appointee and a "Progressive" expert if ever there was one. The Commission was temporarily animated by reform zeal. The approach to decision-making was not legalistic, but the commissioners and staff were in essence living reports of cases, remembering in faithful detail the events of their tenure. Hyneman, I would guess, inferred the application of this approach in the cases of the pre-Maltbie (pre-1930) era also, even though after Stevens' departure in 1913 there is no evidence that the commissioners knew or cared about previously decided cases relevant to an instant case—that is, there is no citation of them in the reports. Hyneman apparently assumed a knowledge of precedents on the part of the post-Stevens commissioners, the lack of citation being put to a desire not to appear overly legalistic. But a look at the hearing minutes, which I can't imagine Hyneman was able to consult, gives the lie to this assumption. What Hyneman gives us, then, is simply a careful cataloguing of reported cases with similar concerns. One uses him as an opening into the hearing minutes and case folders (on microfilm) to see if the commissioners in working up their decisions recognized and made use of analogous cases previously decided. In the Stevens era they did; afterwards they did not. The resulting chaos, I might add, is fully evident in the minutes of the later period.

Also useful in understanding the Commission is an unpublished Ph.D. dissertation, Bruce William Dearstyne's "Railroads and Railroad Regulation in New York State, 1900–1913" (Syracuse University, 1974), a well-researched study that nevertheless misses the point of what Stevens was about in stressing a judicial approach. Like some other studies by historians, and indeed in line with the popular opinion of the Progressive Era, Dearstyne views the judicial approach as a stalling tactic favorable to business interests vis-à-vis the public interest, instead of perhaps the only means of forestalling "capture."

The commissioners themselves, unfortunately, have not left us a great deal. A search of the trade journals and relevant legislative hearings turns up an occasional remark by Stevens or another commissioner, but that is about all.

Index

JACKET DESIGNED BY CAROLINE BECKETT
COMPOSED BY GRAPHIC COMPOSITION, INC.
ATHENS, GEORGIA
MANUFACTURED BY MALLOY LITHOGRAPHING, INC.
ANN ARBOR, MICHIGAN
TEXT AND DISPLAY LINES ARE SET IN CALEDONIA

Library of Congress Cataloging in Publication Data
Chase, William C., 1945–
The American law school and the rise of administrative government.
Bibliography: pp. 165–176.
Includes index.
1. Law schools—United States—History. 2. Law—Study and teaching—United States—History. 3. Administrative law—United States—History. I. Title.
KF272.C42 1982 340'.07'1173 81-69816
ISBN 0-299-09100-7 AACR2